TWR's
Le Mans-winning
JAGUARS

Also from Veloce Publishing

www.veloce.co.uk

First published in October 2020 by Veloce Publishing Limited, Veloce House, Parkway Farm Business Park, Middle Farm Way, Poundbury, Dorchester, Dorset, DT1 3AR, England.
Tel 01305 260068 Fax 01305 250479/e-mail info@veloce.co.uk/web www.veloce.co.uk or www.velocebooks.com.

ISBN: 978-1-787115-68-2 UPC: 6-36847-01568-8

TWR's Le Mans-winning JAGUARS

JOHN STARKEY

VELOCE PUBLISHING
THE PUBLISHER OF FINE AUTOMOTIVE BOOKS

CONTENTS

FOREWORD

Group C racing began in 1982, replacing the previous formula, which had featured Group 5 'silhouette' cars and resulted in almost total domination by the Porsche 935 from 1976, when it was introduced, to 1982, when it was phased out in favour of the new Group C formula.

GTP racing in America began in 1981, and was an effort introduced by John Bishop, then head of IMSA, to break the stranglehold that Porsche had, also with their 935.

Now to the actual cars, which took part in the two series, Group C in Europe and GTP in America.

The most successful car on both sides of the Atlantic, in terms of races won and numbers built, was the Porsche 956/962 family. The 962 was basically a stretched version of the 956, which put the driver's feet behind the centreline of the front wheels, affording at least some protection to them. This had been stipulated in the IMSA rules and once the 962 was introduced in 1985, it dominated the IMSA GTP series, just as the 956 had since its introduction into Group C racing in 1982 in Europe.

If you actually look at the 956/962 family in detail, it's instructive that Porsche didn't start off with the best basics for a ground effect sports car. Its famous 911/930 derived flat-six engine never allowed the engineers (principally Norbert Singer) to build big enough ground effect tunnels into the car itself. By 1987, the Porsches were being beaten by a 'new wave' of sports-prototypes, first of all Jaguars, and then Mercedes. However, there were a lot of Porsche teams in the business of motor racing in those days; they had dominated in the GT era of the 1970s, first with the RSR and then the

turbocharged 'Silhouette' Group 5 formula, which had resulted in the 750 horsepower 200mph-plus 935.

That strength in depth enabled teams such as Joest, Brun and Kremer to still be in with a chance of winning at the end of the 1980s. Indeed, a '962' won at Le Mans as late as 1994, although it was a far cry from the first Rothmans-backed 956s of 1982.

The next car to dominate Group C racing was the TWR Jaguar, particularly in V12-engined form. Whilst a heavy engine, restricted by its single camshaft per bank breathing, the V12 did allow TWR designer Tony Southgate to give his XJRs much bigger ground effect tunnels than the Porsche. Also, Southgate was well in advance of Porsche in chassis design, his cars having chassis made from carbon fibre from the beginning, whilst the Porsches 956/962 design was its first monocoque and still used 'old-fashioned' building materials such as aluminium and steel. Still, it worked, and worked well.

Then we had the Mercedes/Nee Sauber Group C cars of 1986 onward. Neither Sauber nor Mercedes ever claimed that they had the best car in either ground effect or engine technology. Indeed, the chassis was an old-fashioned aluminium and steel monocoque right up to 1990, when the carbon fibre chassis C11 was introduced, but that lightly turbocharged Mercedes V8 engine was a paragon of sheer grunt, allied to reliability.

Through the whole series, companies such as Bosch and Zytec supplied electronic fuel-injection, which became more and more efficient at metering the last drop of available fuel.

Turning now to America, 1981 saw the introduction there of the GTP series. As we have seen, Porsche dominated the IMSA Camel GT Championship in the 1970s, and John Bishop wanted American manufacturers to take more of a part in his series. To that end, he deliberately looked at a type of car able to use American V8 engines, and the rules for the GTP car was the result – in an attempt to break the stranglehold of the Porsche 935.

The first successful 935-beating car was the Lola T600, introduced in 1981. Driven by Brian Redman, it dominated the races, powered by a Chevrolet V8 of $366in^3$, as allowed by the rules. A true ground effect car, it was overtaken in 1983 and '84 by the March series of GTP cars. These were good, workmanlike, tough cars, Adrian Newey's first design, and ideal for a wealthy privateer such as Randy Lanier, the 1984 IMSA Champion. But by 1985 the 962 had arrived and IMSA was once again dominated by Porsche, until the coming of the Electramotive Nissan GTP-ZXT in 1988.

Starting in 1985, this had begun as a Lola T810 ground effect GTP car, still with a chassis made of aluminium and steel. Although the chassis changed for 1988 to a simpler one designed by Trevor Harris – which still used the same basic dimensions as the Lola chassis, but making items such as spring changing much faster and easier – it was still basically the same car, but refined over the years. For 1988, Don Devendorf, a scientist who was also a racer and who oversaw Electramotive, a company that he owned together with John Knepp, had developed an electronically controlled turbocharger wastegate and, fitted with this, Geoff Brabham, sometimes partnered by John Morton, simply ran away with the series, winning nine races outright in 1988, winning the IMSA Championship and repeating the trick three times more in the coming years.

Toyota, in the form of Dan Gurney's California-based team, finally deposed Nissan in the early 1990s, using a lightweight car, the Eagle. By then the series was almost over, which is not to take anything away from them at all. Every single one of the cars and their attendant teams and drivers had to fight fiercely for their success in Group C and IMSA GTP racing.

INTRODUCTION

Jaguars have long competed in racing, beginning in the 1950s with the XK120, then the great Le Mans victories of 1951, '53, and '55-'57 with the C and D types. After the disastrous 1957 fire at its factory in Browns Lane, Coventry, Jaguar retired from active competition, even though it had developed a mid-engined car, the XJ13, which it subsequently cancelled, deciding against competing with Ford, who had recently come onto the scene with its GT40.

It wasn't until the ailing company was reinvigorated by new CEO John Egan, taking it out of British Leyland control in 1984, that Jaguar returned to the arena it had done so well in: World Championship Sports Car/World Sports Prototype Championship (Group C) racing.

John Egan had watched as Jaguar North America had backed a Lee Dykstra-designed, Group 44 run GTP car, the XJR5, and later the XJR7. Although these cars gained an occasional victory, and were usually up with the front running, all-conquering Porsche 962s in American IMSA racing, they were not the success that John Egan was looking for.

In Touring car racing in Europe, a certain Scot, Tom Walkinshaw, had made his name as a good driver and an even better organiser and businessman. He persuaded Jaguar to let him take and develop his own version of their current Grand Touring car, the XJS. With it, Tom Walkinshaw Racing, his race preparation company, won the European Touring Car Championship.

With this as a springboard to gaining the ear of John Egan and Jaguar's other directors, Tom Walkinshaw persuaded them that he, not Bob Tullius, who headed up Group 44 in America, was the right man to lead a Jaguar renaissance in sports car racing. He did, and what follows is the story of what happened ...

FROM MG MIDGET TO TOURING CAR RACING

Tom Walkinshaw was born in 1946, just after the end of the Second World War. His family owned Mauldslie farm, near Penicuik, Midlothian, Scotland, and it would surely not have escaped young Tom that another young man from a Scottish farming family, Jim Clark, had been a Formula One World Champion with Lotus in the 1960s.

Tom Walkinshaw did his first few races in an MG Midget, but in 1968, he began racing a Lotus Formula Ford. He displayed talent, and won the 1969 Scottish Championship, now in a Hawke FF1600.

Graduating to the British Formula Three Championship, Tom began the season in a Lotus before moving to March. This proved to be the wrong choice, and he suffered an accident at Brands Hatch that broke his ankle. After this, Tom drove in Formula Two races, scoring a ninth place with the Ecurie Ecosse team in 1971. He also drove in F5000 races before being hired by Ford for 1974, to drive one of their racing Capris in the British Touring Car Championship. In that year, he won his class and placed fourth overall in the British Saloon Car Championship.

Tom raced in the European Formula 5000 Championship in 1975, but perhaps more importantly, he also started his own race preparation shop in that year: Tom Walkinshaw Racing, based in Kidlington, Oxfordshire, near to the Silverstone race circuit. Its first job was modifying BMW 3.0 CSLs, the company Tom had signed with for 1976. That year, Tom had shared a BMW CSL coupe with John Fitzpatrick in the Silverstone six hours. Tom did the opening stint and then left John

to drive for over four hours to win the race and collect the trophy, whilst he flew from Northamptonshire to Thruxton, where he raced a Capri and scored his second win in one day.

John Fitzpatrick: "I got to know Tom in the mid 1970s when we shared a few touring car races together. He had the 'Hermetite' sponsored BMW CSL, and he and I used to share the car, we would do pretty much the same lap times as each other and we won a few races. The Silverstone six hours in 1976 comes to mind. I drove over four hours there and we won. But not only was Tom a good driver, he was a very good organiser as well.

"Tom always paid well. His staff were all good, he only hired the best people and he paid them well too, which isn't always the case in motor racing. I remember in the early 1980s, he asked me to a meeting at his fabulous manor house that he lived in on the estate where he had his business. Tom asked me to drive his Jaguar XJS with him and offered me twice as much as anyone else would for the drive. He always used to pay up front too, not after the race, as most other team bosses did."

Results like the win at Silverstone in 1976 led to the Mazda factory contracting TWR to run its RX-7s in the British Touring Car Championship and, with Win Percy driving, TWR-Mazda won the championship in 1980 and 1981. It had been second in 1979.

TWR developed Rover Vitesses, as well as the Mazdas, for the British Saloon Car Championship, winning 11 out of 11 races in 1983, but the team was

Steve Soper and René Metge winning the RAC Tourist Trophy in a TWR-prepared Rover Vitesse in 1983.
(Courtesy Graham Robson)

The TWR-prepared
Rover Vitesse today.
(Author's collection)

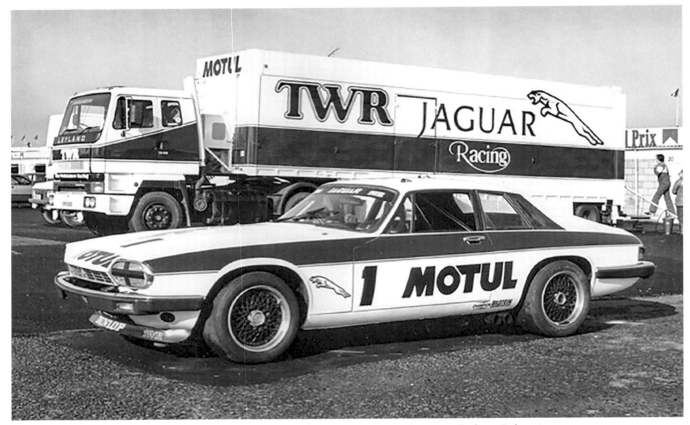

The TWR Equipe, together with its XJ-S in 1983. (Courtesy Graham Robson)

stripped of its title for 'Technical infringements'(!). It would not be the last time that the team had interpreted the rules a little too loosely ...

Meanwhile, the year before, TWR had come to an agreement with Jaguar, which saw TWR enter the 5.3-litre V12-engined Jaguar XJS coupe in 1984 in the prestigious European Touring Car Championship.

TWR now had Motul Oils sponsorship, and the team concentrated on lightening the XJS extensively. In fact, it almost got the race car down to the minimum permissible weight of 1400kg, reaching 1435kg in 1983.

Eager to include the Jaguar in what were usually BMW-dominated races, the series organisers were keen to have the TWR team attend with the XJS. This, despite the fact that TWR used a few 'modifications' on its car. For instance, the cabin requirements were such that supposedly four people would be able to sit in it. After

all, these were touring car races. So TWR relocated the rear bulkhead further back than on the standard car, to fulfil this rule.

The TWR XJS also had outboard rear disc brakes, instead of the original inboard braking. The bag fuel tank system was 'massaged' to get longer runs in between pit stops, and centre lock wheels, instead of the usual five-bolt wheel fixing, made wheel changes much faster.

Also, the regulations for Group A, which the touring cars ran under, specified that 5000 cars to a similar specification had to be produced each year, and the TWR XJ-S certainly never fulfilled that rule.

This ingenious rule interpretation often attracted complaints from rivals, plus occasional race disqualifications, and a protest that eventually ended in the British High Court.

Allan Scott, in charge of engine development for TWR

12th June 1983. Tom Walkinshaw and Win Percy won the Czechoslovakian Grand Prix at Brno in their Group A Jaguar XK-S, prepared by Tom Walkinshaw Racing. (Courtesy Graham Robson)

did a great job for the team. In the 1982 season, the TWR XJS's engine developed some 390 horsepower. For 1983 it developed 420 to 430 horsepower, and maximum rpm was now at 7250 instead of the previous year's 6500.

Cosworth was brought in by TWR in 1984, and new camshafts gave the engine 485-490 horsepower at 8000 rpm.

In 1984, TWR and Jaguar won the Spa 24-hour race and both the driver and manufacturer titles of the European Touring Car Championship. But Tom Walkinshaw had his mind set on greater things ...

2

JAGUAR XJR-5 AND XJR-7 (GROUP 44)

Bob Tullius. (Courtesy Graham Robson)

Bob Tullius was an American racing enthusiast and driver, who liked cars from Britain. To that end, he formed the Group 44 racing team in the early 1960s with Brian Fuerstenau as his partner. Apart from the Howmet Turbine car in 1968, he campaigned Jaguar E-types, MGs and Triumph TR8s in the United States over the next 20 years.

Having driven the Howmet Turbine car at Le Mans, Bob Tullius vowed to return there one day with a car of his own. The result was the Jaguar XJR-5, designed by Lee Dykstra, and built to compete mainly in the IMSA Championship in America, even though Tullius also intended for it to run at Le Mans.

Mike Dale, the head of Jaguar Cars Inc of New Jersey, was persuaded to finance the project, and he engaged Dykstra to design the ground effect semi-monocoque car, the chassis of which was built from aluminium honeycomb.

At this time, Jaguar had managed to extract itself from the clutches of the British Leyland organisation, and was now headed up in England by a new CEO, John Egan, who was determined to give Jaguar a fresher, more modern image which, he believed, with proper quality control of their range of road cars, would bring the company back into profit. Mike Dale was of the same opinion, and believed that success in IMSA and Le Mans could be worth sales of over 200 more cars per year in the US.

By January 1982, drawings and clay models of the new car were being publicised on a wide scale.

The new car's design was a sheet aluminium

A Group 44 XJR-5. (Courtesy Graham Robson)

monocoque, with a honeycomb floor section and steel bulkheads reinforced with steel tubing.

There were ground effect venturi running from behind the flat-bottom cockpit area alongside the fully-stressed V12 engine block, curving upwards towards the rear to exit under the rear wing. Kevlar and carbon fibre were used in the make up of the bodywork and the suspension used double wishbones front and rear ad featured the rear coil/damper units mounted high above the upper wishbone to give an uncluttered exit for the airflow.

Summit Point saw the prototype XJR-5 being tested in June 1982, and it had its first race at the very fast Road America circuit in Wisconsin in August. There, Bob Tullius and Bill Adam finished third behind two Porsche 935s, and they were the first GTP finishers. After this, results were harder to come by for the rest of the season.

John Egan, the chairman of Jaguar, stands proudly by the Group 44 Jaguar at Daytona in 1983. (Courtesy Graham Robson)

Dykstra began a gradual refinement of the car from 1983, and, by the summer of 1985, '99.9 percent' of the original parts had been redrawn. Lighter weight and better aerodynamics were the result, and the V12 engine, which had been on carburettors, went from 5.3 litres to 6, as well as getting Lucas/Micos engine management for 1984.

Brian Redman, Bill Adam and Pat Bedard drove this XJR-5 to 24th place at the 1984 Daytona 24 hours. (Courtesy Lee Self)

Tullius and Adam won at Road Atlanta in '83, and more wins came at Lime Rock, Mosport and Pocono (Tullius and 'Doc' Bundy). Bob Tullius came second to Al Holbert in the Drivers' Championship that year.

In 1984, at Miami for the three hours, the two cars, now fitted with Lucas Electronic fuel-injection, finished first and second, driven by Brian Redman/'Doc' Bundy and Bob Tullius/Pat Bedard. After this, there were five second places and two third places that season. The 'Blue Thunder' March 83G/84Gs, driven by Randy Lanier, who became that year's champion, and Bill Whittington proved to be the superior package.

One XJR-5 had been flown to Silverstone in mid-1983, and tested in May by Derek Bell, who gave a favourable report to John Egan to back Group 44's plans for an entry at Le Mans for 1984. The car was two seconds slower per lap than the winning Porsche 956 had been at Silverstone shortly before this test. Bob Tullius also drove the car there, but Tom Walkinshaw, whose company, TWR was by then supplying Jaguar V12 engines to Group 44, was not allowed to drive it.

Although the two cars looked immaculate and

Daytona 24 hours, 1984. Bob Tullius, David Hobbs and Doc Bundy drove their Group 44 XJR-5 into third place. (Courtesy Lee Self)

impressed all who saw them at Le Mans, they were slower than the many Porsche 956s there, and both cars retired before the end of the race – one driven by Claude

Ballot-Lena crashed when a tyre deflated, and the other had a gearbox problem, although it did actually cross the finish line. The gearbox problem would trouble the cars until the Hewland VG boxes were replaced with VGC ones in 1986.

Another problem rarely highlighted when discussing the differences between IMSA racing in America and Le Mans racing in France, is the fuel. Specifically, in America, the engines could consume very high octane fuel, and drink as much of it as they could take. In France, the octane rating of the fuel was much lower, so engine ignition timing, and perhaps even the compression ratio, had to be scaled back. This resulted in a power loss for the American entered Jaguars, as compared to their performance "back home."

1985 saw the new Porsche 962s winning regularly in IMSA, and the XJRs had just a single win at Road Atlanta with Brian Redman and Hurley Haywood driving and several good finishes. At Le Mans that year, Bob Tullius, Chip Robinson and Claude Ballot-Lena finished 13th with a sick engine, while the second car broke a driveshaft.

Earlier that year, another XJR-5 had been sent to Jaguar, which had given it to TWR to install its four camshaft V12 engine. The car was repainted in British Racing Green with 'Jaguar' picked out in white on the nose and sides. In March, it was tested at Silverstone, with Martin Brundle driving, and later, at Donington.

In his excellent book *TWR and Jaguar V12 Prototype Sports Cars*, Alan Scott, the head of the engine department at TWR, wrote that the four-valve, 6.2-litre engine was giving some 686bhp at 7000rpm at this test, and was using the Lucas Micos engine management system that Jaguar wanted to use, against Scott's desire to use the new Zytec system. Scott found that dealing with a small company, such as Zytec was at that time, was far easier in terms of decision making than with the Lucas company.

The Jaguar V12 engine, as installed in the Group 44 Jaguar XJR-5. (Courtesy Jerri Self)

The well appointed cockpit of the Group 44 XJR-5.
(Courtesy Jerri Self)

At the end of 1985, the XJR-7 appeared at the Daytona 3 hours driven by Chip Robinson and Bob Tullius. The signs were hopeful. The XJR-7 resembled the XJR-5, but it was lighter, had more downforce and less drag. The chassis floor and sides were now of machined aluminium, and composite materials were used extensively. Suspension was lightened, and the steering effort was lighter. A 6.5-litre engine, developing 700 horsepower, was now fitted.

Back in England, due to his success with the XJ-S touring car programme, Tom Walkinshaw had been asked by John Egan to build and run a British-built Jaguar Group C car. TWR evaluated an XJR-5 in early 1985. TWR installed their own 48-valve engine, but Walkinshaw told Jaguar management that he did not want to use the American-made car as it did not have enough downforce for Group C racing. Having been given the go-ahead by Jaguar Management, he employed Tony Southgate to design the new XJR-6 for its WEC debut in 1986.

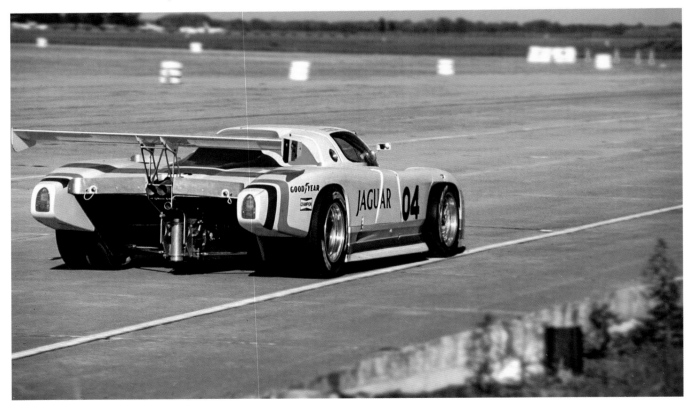

The number 04 Group 44 Jaguar XJR-7 at Sebring for the March 1986 12-hour race was driven by Hurley Haywood, Vern Schuppan and Brian Redman. It retired after 146 laps. It is seen here braking for turn one. (Courtesy Lee Self)

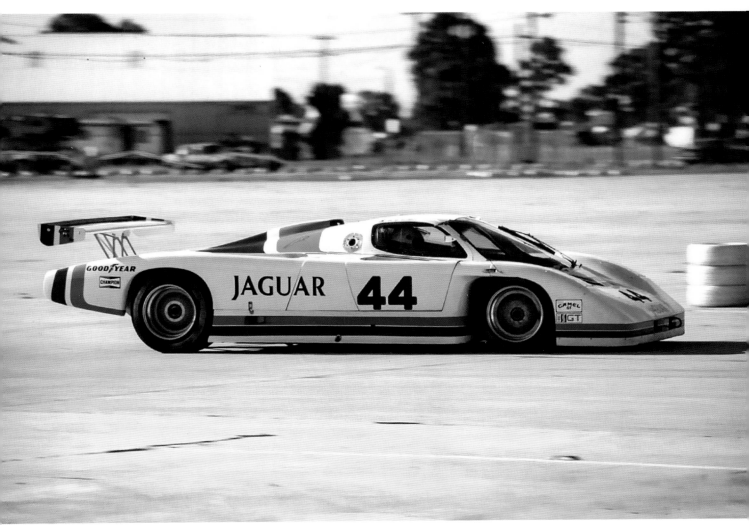

The sister car, #44, XJR-7 at Sebring in 1986. Driven by Bob Tullius and Chip Robinson, it finished in fourth place.
(Courtesy Lee Self)

Hurley Haywood and Chip Robinson drove their XJR-7 to third place at Mid-Ohio in June, 1986.

The last hurrah. 1988 Daytona 24 hours and the number 66 XJR-8 of Eddie Cheever, Johnny Dumfries and John Watson, chassis number 188, sweeps past the Group 44 XJR-7 on its way to third place. This was the last time the Group 44 Jaguar raced in IMSA. (Courtesy Lee Self)

For the 1986 Daytona 24 hours, Group 44 had its new XJR-7, and managed a creditable sixth place, but it was not until the final 3-hour race at Daytona in December that it won its only race of the year, with Bob Tullius and Chip Robinson driving. At the end of 1986, Jaguar/Group 44 had scored enough points to come second to Porsche in the 1986 manufacturers' table.

With TWR in England now employed as Jaguar's main 'works' team, Tullius's brave Group 44 effort finished at the end of 1987, when Jaguar withdrew its financial support. They won twice in 1987, however, at Riverside and West Palm Beach: both times with Haywood and John Morton driving.

Despite not having factory backing, the 1988 Daytona 24 hours saw not only the debut of the TWR XJR-9 GTP car, but also an XJR-7 entry, driven by Bob Tullius, Hurley Haywood and Whitney Ganz. It retired on Saturday evening with a failed cylinder-head gasket.

Constructor	Group 44, Victory Lane, Winchester, Virginia, USA
Chassis fabricator	Dave Klym (Fabcar)
Chassis	Semi-monocoque sheet aluminium, with honeycomb floor panel and tubular reinforced steel bulkheads, designed by Lee Dykstra. Ground effect car. Twin side-mounted Alan Docking water radiators, single side-mounted Setraub oil radiator. 27 gallon mid-mounted fuel tank, single 4 gallon oil tank in left side-pod.
Body	Kevlar and carbon fibre panels
Engine	Jaguar 60 degree V12 (modified by John Huber) naturally aspirated, liquid cooled 90.0 x 70.0mm/5343cc

Aluminium block and heads
Stressed chassis member
Wet cast iron liners
7 plain main bearings
Steel crankshaft with harmonic damper
Steel con rods
Hepworth light alloy 3-ring pistons
SOHC – single duplex chain driven
2 titanium valves/cylinder, 1 plug
Lucas Opus ignition, 6 Weber carburettors*
Borg & Beck 3-plate clutch
570bhp at 6900rpm
Weight 240kg approx

* Lucas Micos engine management and Bosch solenoid injection fitted to 6.0 and 6.5-litre (XJR-7) versions.

Suspension   Upper and lower wishbones, Koni coil/damper units and anti-roll bars front and rear. Rear coil/dampers mounted above upper wishbones at the rear to clear the venturi tunnels.

Cast iron ventilated discs with AP 4-pot calipers outboard. Jongbloed 15in rims (later 16in) – 11.5in wide front, 14in rear. Goodyear tyres.

Gearbox and reverse   Hewland VG5-200 5-speed

Dimensions   Wheelbase – 2756mm
Front track – 1676mm
Rear track – 1575mm
Weight   930kg
Top Speed   190mph

Note: Apart from the Le Mans and Daytona results shown below, the IMSA results are speculative as Group 44 did not keep detailed records (so the author was informed by Bob Tullius on 16th June, 2005).

XJR5 – 001   1982 – GTP   Group 44/Bob Tullius

1982:
22/08: Road America Pabst 500: Bob Tullius/Bill Adam, #44; 1st
05/09: Mid Ohio Lumberman's 6-hour: Tullius/Adam, #44; DNS (Crash in practice)

1983:
01/05: Monterey Triple Crown, Laguna Seca: B Tullius, #44; 2nd

The car was held as a spare throughout the rest of 1983, then set aside as continuing development in suspension design and weight reduction made it obsolete. The car was exhibited at the 2000 Goodwood Festival of Speed, driven by Bob Tullius.

XJR5 – 002   GTP   Group 44/Bob Tullius

1982:
26/09/82: Pocono: B Tullius, #44; DNF (engine)
28/11: Daytona: B Tullius, #44; DNF (suspension)

1983:
31/1-01/02: Daytona: B Tullius/B Adam, #44; DNF
25/02: Miami: B Tullius/B Adam, #44; 5thOA
25/03: Sebring 12 Hrs: B Tullius/B Adam, #44; DNF
10/04: Road Atlanta: B Tullius/B Adam, #44; 1stOA
24/04: Riverside: B Tullius/B Adam, #44;
30/05: Lime Rock: B Tullius/B Adam, #44; 1stOA
31/07: Portland: B Tullius/B Adam, #44; DNF (acc. damage)
14/08: Mosport: B Tullius/B Adam, #44; 1stOA
11/09: Pocono: B Tullius/D Bundy, #44; 1stOA

XJR5 – 003   GTP   Group 44/Bob Tullius

1984:
26/02: Miami GP: B Tullius/P Bedard, #44, 2ndOA
08/04: Road Atlanta: B Tullius/D Bundy, #44; DNF
20/05: Charlotte: B Tullius/D Bundy, #44; 2ndOA
08/07: Watkins Glen: B Tullius/D Bundy, #44; DNF
29/07: Portland: B Tullius/D Bundy, #44; 2ndOA
05/08: Sears Point: D Bundy, #44; 2nd
26/08: Road America: B Tullius/D Bundy, #44; 18th
09/09: Pocono: B Tullius/D Bundy, #44; 2ndOA OA
16/09: Michigan: B Tullius/D Bundy, #44; DNF
30/09: Watkins Glen: B, Tullius, #44; DNF
25/11: Daytona: B Tullius/D Bundy, #44; DNF

XJR5 – 004   GTP   Group 44

1984:
26/02: Miami GP: B Redman/D Bundy, #04; 1stOA
08/04: Road Atlanta: B Redman/P Bedard, #04; 3rdOA
20/05: Charlotte: B Redman/P Bedard, #04; 3rdOA

08/07: Watkins Glen: B Redman/P Bedard, #04; 3rdOA
29/07: Portland: B Redman/H Haywood, #04; 8thOA
05/08: Sears Point: B Redman, #04; 3rdOA
26/08: Road America: B Redman/H Haywood, #04; 5thOA
09/09: Pocono: B Redman/H Haywood, #04; DNF
16/09: Michigan: B Redman/H Haywood, #04; 20thNR
30/09: Watkins Glen: B Redman/H Haywood, #04; DNF
25/10: Daytona: B Redman/H Haywood, #04; 2ndOA

1985:
14/04: Road Atlanta: B Redman/H Haywood, #04; 1stOA

XJR5 – 005   1984 GTP   Group 44/Bob Tullius

1984:
24/03: Sebring 12 hours: B Redman/J Adams/H Haywood, #04; 11thOA (pole)

XJR5 – 006   1984 GTP   Group 44/Bob Tullius

1984:
24/03: Sebring 12 hours: B Tullius/P Bedard, #44, DNF
16-17/06: Le Mans 24 hours: B Tullius/B Redman/D Bundy, #44; NRF
Sold to Jaguar/TWR Racing

1985:
15-16/06: Le Mans 24 hours: B Tulles/C Robinson/C Ballot-Lena, #44; 13thOA/1st in IMSA class
2000: Sold to JD Classics
2005: Auctioned

XJR5 – 007   GTP   Group 44/Bob Tullius

Possibly:
1985:
24/02: Miami: B Redman, #44; DNF
14/04: Road Atlanta: B Tullius/C Robinson, #44; 2ndOA
28/04: Riverside: B Tullius/C Robinson, #44; 3rdOA
05/05: Laguna Seca: B Tullius/C Robinson, #44; 2ndOA
19/05: Charlotte: B Tullius/C Robinson, #44; 4thOA
27/05: Lime Rock: B Tullius/C Robinson, #44; 4thOA.
09/06: Mid-Ohio: B Tullius/C Robinson, #44; 4thOA
28/07: Portland: B Tullius/C Robinson, #44; 4thOA
04/08: Sears Point: B Tullius/C Robinson, #44; DNF

25/08: Road America: B Tullius/C Robinson, #44; DNF
08/09: Pocono: B Tullius, #44; DNF
29/09: Watkins Glen 2: B Tullius/C Robinson, #44; 6thOA
06/10: Columbus: B Tullius/C Robinson, #44; DNF

XJR5 – 008   1985 GTP   Group 44/Bob Tullius

1984:
04-05/02: Daytona 24 hours: B Tullius/D Hobbs/D Bundy, #44; 3rdOA
16-17/6: Le Mans 24 hours:T Adamowicz/J Watson/C Ballot-Lena, #40; DNF

1985:
Possibly:
02-03/02: Daytona 24 hours: B Tullius/B Redman, #44; DNF
15-16/6: Le Mans 24 hours: B Redman/J Adams/H Haywood, #40; DNF (driveshaft)
23/03: Sebring 12 hours: B Tullius/C Robinson, #44; 4thOA
Sold to Duncan Hamilton

XJR5 – 009   GTP   Group 44/Bob Tullius

1985:
25/02: Miami: H Haywood/C Robinson, #04; 4thOA
05/05: Laguna Seca: B Redman/H Haywood, #04; 3rdOA
19/05: Charlotte: B Redman/H Haywood, #04; 2ndOA
27/05: Lime Rock: B Redman/H Haywood, #04; 2ndOA
08/07: Watkins Glen: B Redman/H Haywood, #04; 2ndOA
28/07: Portland: B Redman/H Haywood, #04; 4thOA
04/08: Sears Point: B Redman/H Haywood, #04; DNF
25/08: Road America: B Redman/H Haywood, #04; 8thOA
08/09: Pocono:C Robinson/H Haywood, #04; 2ndOA
29/9: Watkins Glen 2: B Redman/H Haywood, #04; 2ndOA
06/10: Columbus: B Redman/H Haywood, #04; DNF
01/12: Daytona: B Redman/H Haywood, #04; 2ndOA

XJR5 – 010   GTP   Group 44/Bob Tullius

1984:
29/07: Portland 500 KM: Tullius /Bundy, #44; 2nd
05/08: Sears Point: Tullius/Bundy, #44; 2nd
09/09: Pocono Camel GT 500: Bundy, #44; 2nd
16/09: Michigan 500 KM: Tullius/Bundy, #44; 11th
30/09: Watkins Glen 500 KM: Tullius, #44; DNF (gearbox)

10/12: 24-hour Daytona test: Tullius/Aase /Haywood/Robinson /Redman
1985:
24/02: Miami Grand Prix: Tullius/Redman, #44; DNF gearbox
23/03: Sebring 12 hours: Tullius /Robinson, #44; 4th
15-16/06: Le Mans 24 hours: Back up car
28/07: Portland 300 KM: Tullius /Robinson, #44; 2nd
29/09: Watkins Glen 500 KM: Tullius/Robinson, #44; 6th
05/10: Columbus 500 KM: Tullius /Robinson, #44; DNF (gearbox)

Last XJR-5 built, used for press rides and shows in 1986 and 1987

XJR5 – 011   GTP

Built up later from spares
Sold to Walter Hill - Never raced
2005: Sold

XJR5 – 012   GTP

Built from spares
Never raced

XJR7 – 001   GTP   Group 44/Bob Tullius

1985:
01/12: Daytona finale: Tullius/Robinson, #44; 4th

1986:
14/04: Charlotte Tire test: Robinson, #44; crash, repair
26/05: Lime Rock: H Haywood, #04; DNF
08/06: Mid-Ohio: B Redman/H Haywood, #04; 5thOA
22/06: W Palm Beach: B Redman/H Haywood, #04;3rdOA
06/07: Watkins Glen 1: B Redman/H Haywood, #04; DNF
27/07: Portland: B Redman/H Haywood, #04; 9thOA
03/08: Sears Point: B Redman/H Haywood, #04;3rdOA
24/08: Road America: B Redman/H Haywood, #04; DNF
26/10: Daytona: B Redman/H Haywood, #04; DNF

1987:
01/03: Miami: H Haywood/J Morton, #44; 10thOA
03/05: Laguna Seca: H Haywood/J Morton, #44; 4th
25/03: Lime Rock: J Morton/H Haywood, #44; 5th

21/06: W Palm Beach: H Haywood/J Morton, #44; 1stOA
05/07: Watkins Glen 1: B Tullius/J Morton, #44; 13thOA
25/10: San Diego: H Haywood/J Morton, #44; 10th

1988:
31/01-01/02: 24 hours of Daytona: H Haywood/W Ganz/B Tullius, #44; 61stNR
1997: Sold to James Rogers

XJR7 – 002   GTP   Group 44/Bob Tullius

1986:
02-03/02: Sunbank 24 at Daytona: Hurley Haywood/Brian Redman/Vern Schuppan, #04 DNF (motor)
03/02: Miami Grand Prix: Redman/Haywood, #04; 4th
22/03: Sebring 12 hours:Redman/Haywood/Schuppan,#04; DNF (motor)
06/04: Road Atlanta: Redman/Haywood, #04; DNF (motor)
27/04: Riverside: Redman/Haywood, #04; DNF (motor)
04/05: Laguna Seca: Robinson/Haywood, #44; 2nd
15-16/6: Le Mans 24 hours: B Tullius/C Robinson/C Ballot-Lena, #44; 13thOA/1st IMSA GTP
24/08: Road America: Redman/Haywood, #04; DNF (trans)
21/09: Watkins Glen: Redman/Haywood, #04; 5th
05/10: Columbus: Redman/Haywood, #04; 3rd
26/10: Daytona Finale: Tullius/Robinson, #44;1st

Still with Mr Tullius

XJR7 – 003   GTP   Group 44/Bob Tullius

Possibly:
1986:
02/03: Miami: B Tullius/C Robinson, #44; DNF
06/04: Road Atlanta: B Tullius/C Robinson, #44; 4thOA
27/04: Riverside: B Tullius/C Robinson, #44; DNF
04/05: Laguna Seca: C Robinson/H Haywood, #44; 2ndOA
26/05: Lime Rock: B Tullius/C Robinson, #44; 5thOA
08/06: Mid-Ohio: B Tullius/C Robinson, #44; 2ndOA
22/06: W Palm Beach: B Tullius/C Robinson, #44; 10thOA
06/07: Watkins Glen 1: B Tullius/C Robinson, #44; 9thOA
27/07: Portland: B Tullius/C Robinson, #44; 2ndOA
03/08: Sears Point: B Tullius/C Robinson, #44; DNF
24/08: Road America: B Tullius/C Robinson, #44; DNF
21/09: Watkins Glen 2: B Tullius/C Robinson, #44; 14thOA
05/10: Columbus: B Tullius/C Robinson, #44; DNF

26/10: Daytona: B Tullius/C Robinson, #44; 1stOA

Riverside: Crashed in testing

1987:
1-2/2: Daytona 24 hours: B Tullius/H Haywood/J Morton, #44; DNF
26/10: Riverside: H Haywood/J Morton, #44; 1stOA

XJR7 – 004   GTP   Group 44/Bob Tullius

1986:
02/02: Sunbank 24 at Daytona: Bob Tullius/Chip Robinson, Claude Ballot-Lena, #44; 6th

02/03: Miami Grand Prix: Bob Tullius/Chip Robinson, #44; DNF (clutch)
22/03: Sebring 12 hours: Tullius/Robinson/Ballot-Lena, #44 DNF (belt)
06/04: Road Atlanta: Tullius/Robinson, #44; 4th
27/04: Riverside: Tullius/Robinson, #44; DNF (crash)

Still with Mr Tullius

XJR7 – 005   GTP   Group 44/Bob Tullius

Still with Mr Tullius, the 'Mag Jag'

Another view of the Jaguar V12 engine, as used in the Group 44 Jaguar GTP cars. (Courtesy Jerri Self)

Chapter 3

JAGUAR XJR-6 (TOM WALKINSHAW RACING)

The new TWR XJR-6s collected a crowd wherever they appeared. Resplendent in their British Racing green/white paintwork, they were amongst the best designed and built cars of their day. This is the car driven by Hans Heyer and Jan Lammers at Brands Hatch in 1985, in the pits. Chassis number 285. The XJR-6 was the only TWR car to have gullwing doors. (Courtesy John S Allen)

Once Tom Walkinshaw had been given the green light by Jaguar management, in the form of John Egan, to design and develop a Jaguar contender for Group C racing, his first step was to hire Tony Southgate in autumn, 1984. Southgate had recent experience in designing Group C cars in the shape of the 1982 Ford C100, and he was to remain TWR's designer up to 1989.

Rather than continuing to use aluminium composites, as the Lee Dykstra design for Group 44 had, Tony Southgate designed the chassis and body for the new XJR-6 to be built out of carbon fibre and Kevlar. The bulkhead between the engine compartment and the cockpit was recessed by 11cm, in order to allow the long V12 engine to be mounted as far forward as possible. The first design featured no less than three fuel tanks, although that would change in the XJR-8 to a single 99-litre bag tank. Alan Scott was, as we have seen, TWR's

engine developer, and he built the engines from part-machined V12 blocks (these were the only major 'Jaguar' components in the whole car), and in-house/sub-contract fabricated parts, some from Cosworth engineering.

The rear suspension's design, in particular, was governed by the two large ground effect venturis, which ran along either side of the 60 degree V12 engine. A cast aluminium beam was bolted to the gearbox casing and the Koni damper/coil spring unit was suspended to this, linking to the lower wide based wishbones, which were also attached to the gearbox casing at their inner ends. Rear wheel diameter was 19in.

At the front, the suspension used pushrod operated coil spring/damper units, mounted almost horizontal, from a casting made from magnesium. A very stiff anti-roll bar was employed to counteract the weight of the big V12 engine. The disc brakes were cross drilled and used

Side view of 285 racing, showing the cowled-in rear wheels and the side skirts, all to help the cars develop enormous amounts of downforce. (Courtesy John S Allen)

The TWR Jaguar XJR-6 in its first year, when competing at Brands Hatch. Race #51 was driven by Alan Jones and Jean-Louis Schlesser. Sadly, it retired with engine failure, as did the sister car, race #52, driven by Hans Heyer and Jan Lammers. (Courtesy John S Allen)

four-pot AP calipers. The March gearbox was bolted to a TWR-made bellhousing.

Jaguar's 6.2-litre V12 engine, in TWR/Cosworth form with single overhead camshaft per bank and 2 valves per cylinder, was now developing some 660 horsepower plus and development was always ongoing in the attempt to find more power and torque. As Group C was primarily a fuel formula, meaning that fuel mileage was critical, finding more power, without increasing consumption, was the key to winning. The bodywork of

the new XJ6 was also in carbon fibre and Kevlar, and the weight of the prototype was just over 900kg.

Where the new XJR-6 differed from its Group C contemporaries was in the design of its ground effect underside. In experiments that Tony Southgate carried out in October 1984, in the Imperial College wind tunnel in London, he discovered that using full length venturis could actually unbalance the Ford C100. Southgate also discovered at this time that the slipstream flowing along the sides of the car was being sucked in

XJR-6, chassis number 185, at Druids Hairpin, Brands Hatch in September, 1985. (Courtesy John S Allen)

and contributing to the air coming from beneath the nose, thereby disturbing the airflow when it encountered the diffuser. So the XJR-6 was designed with a flat front underbody section, which led to the large tunnels that started at the rear of the cockpit floor. To control the air, both at the nose and at the sides, splitters were employed and the XJR-6 could actually be set up so that the nose splitter could rub on the tarmac if necessary. Behind the diffuser, Southgate designed a large rear wing, which helped to extract the air rushing out of the diffuser.

Around the rear wheels, 'spats' were fitted in an attempt to stop air escaping and to direct the maximum

possible airflow into the venturis. Around the front wheels, the flat bottom was tailored to closely fit them, only allowing for steering movement. At 180mph, there was 5000lb of downforce, giving the XJR-6 by far the most downforce of any Group C car up to 1985. By careful design, Southgate was also able to keep the centre of pressure well forward of the mid point of the car, this also helping its stability.

So efficient was the design of the aerodynamics that, as Martin Brundle explained in his interview with *Motorsport* in July 2019: "I'd go out," remembers Martin, "come back and say: 'The floor's not right.' You could feel it straight away, because you'd go into a corner and like, 'Whoa! The floor's not right' and the team would say, 'The floor's fine' and you'd say, 'No it isn't' and then they'd get under the car and be, like, 'OK, yeah, the floor wasn't quite right.' As soon as it was perfectly aligned, the car would just hunker down."

The dark green TWR Jaguars, sponsorless and with only the name 'Jaguar' in white appearing on the nose and flanks, first appeared at Snetterton in early July, with Martin Brundle and Mike Thackwell doing the test driving. Hans Heyer was also attending the test. The Group 44 XJR-5 was also there, still fitted with the four-valve per cylinder heads on its TWR-built V12 engine, to see how much faster the new Tony Southgate-designed XJR-6 was.

This was purely a shakedown test, and more serious testing was carried out at Donington on July 30th, to see how the new car did with the Group C fuel amount

The programme for the Spa 1000km made great play of the new Group C Jaguar. (Courtesy John Gabrial)

Porsche bien sûr, mais aussi Lancia et... Jaguar !

C'était en 1964, le Royal Automobile Club de Spa organisait sa première course d'endurance. Il s'agissait d'une épreuve disputée sur 500 km par une chaleur accablante.
Mike Parkes, au volant de sa Ferrari, franchissait la ligne d'arrivée en vainqueur remportant la course à plus de 200 km/h de moyenne.
Ce week-end, vingt et un ans après, que de choses ont changé.
L'épreuve du RAC Spa se dispute sur 1.000 km, les Ferrari ont disparu du plateau, et bien que les voitures soient devenues beaucoup plus performantes, la moyenne ne dépassera pas les 200 km/h, il est vrai que les 14 kilomètres de l'ancien tracé, très rapide, ont été abandonnés au profit d'une piste longue de la moitié mais beaucoup plus technique et n'autorisant plus des vitesses de plus de 250 km/h de moyenne au tour.
Cette année les 1.000 km de Spa constituent la septième manche du championnat du monde d'endurance, un championnat dominé depuis

quatre ans par Porsche.
Le constructeur allemand s'est en effet approprié les 3 derniers titres mondiaux, et cette année il n'en sera pas autrement.
Toutefois si le titre ne pourra lui échapper, on ne sait encore si celui-ci, reviendra à l'usine ou à un de ses clients.
Depuis le début de la saison, si les pilotes officiels l'ont emporté à Mugello grâce à Jacky Ickx et Jochen Mass, à Silverstone à nouveau avec Jacky Ickx et Mass, et à Hockenheim avec Derek Bell et Hans-Stuck, à Monza par contre Surer-Winkelhock imposèrent une Porsche-client, alors qu'au Mans, c'était le trio composé de Ludwig-Barilla-Winter qui montait sur la plus haute marche du podium à l'issue d'une course de 24 heures qu'ils dominèrent pratiquement de bout en bout leur Porsche-client...
Cette saison, plus que jamais, les voitures d'usine ne sont plus imbattables. Si pour les 1.000 km de Spa elles partiront avec la cote de favorites, ayant remporté les trois dernières éditions, les

nombreuses autres Porsches-privées ne s'annoncent pas moins comme de redoutables concurrentes.
Mais, au delà de la lutte que ne manqueront pas de se livrer les différents équipages défendant les couleurs du constructeur allemand, ces 1.000 km de Spa pourraient aussi nous valoir une surprise.
Les Lancia, rapides mais tenant difficilement la distance, ne cessent de se rapprocher des premières places.
Alors qui sait...
Francorchamps sera également l'occasion pour les toutes nouvelles Jaguar de Tom Walkinshaw de démontrer leur potentiel.
D'autant que le circuit ardennais réussit généralement très bien au préparateur britannique.
Enfin cette année, plus que jamais le paramètre consommation a pris une place importante et est une des composantes sinon déterminantes du moins très importantes pour la victoire.
Rappelons que pour ces 1.000 km de Spa les

voitures du groupe C1 ne pourront pas utiliser plus de 510 litres de ce précieux carburant, les C2 étant même limitées à ... 330 litres !
Pour ce sprint de 6 heures il faudra impérativement résoudre l'équation : aller vite, mais sans consommer de trop.
Telles sont les données de départ, reste maintenant à faire votre pronostic.
Porsche bien sûr, mais pourquoi pas Lancia ou ... Jaguar ?
À moins que...
Mais place maintenant à la course, au suspense.
Un suspense de 6 heures, et pour le vivre pleinement ne vous limiter pas à la ligne droite des stands, à la Source ou au Raidillon, profitez-en pour découvrir les nombreux autres endroits spectaculaires de ce circuit de Spa-Francorchamps.
Les 1.000 km vous offrent cette très belle occasion !

Jean-Marc Hardy.

Another view of 285 at Brands Hatch in 1985. (Courtesy John S Allen)

allocated. The target was 1.592 litres per lap over 86 laps, but the car averaged 1.64 litres, slightly over the target. However, the gearing was not quite right for the circuit, and the car was troubled by understeer, which certainly did not help fuel consumption

There was another test at Silverstone, before the car was shipped out to Canada for its first race there, and Mike Thackwell came within 0.5 second of the lap record for sports cars, and so the team knew that they had a competitive car on their hands.

The Mosport 1000km was in August, 1985 and despite Porsche 962s heading the grid, it was Martin Brundle who beat them to the first corner, leading for the first nine laps but retiring on the 13th after a wheel bearing had failed. Jean-Louis Schlesser in the other car, later on

joined by Martin Brundle and Mike Thackwell, finished third, a good result for a first time out with the new car. Sadly, this race saw Manfred Winkelhock sustain fatal injuries when his Porsche 962 crashed.

At Spa, Brundle and Thackwell were fifth but, as this was the race at which Stefan Bellof was killed in another accident in a Porsche 962, it was almost academic, as the race itself was stopped after 122 laps.

Brands Hatch saw the TWR team struggling, with one car retiring with broken valve springs, whilst the other suffered from jammed throttle slides and also retired.

John Fitzpatrick: "I remember the first time that TWR brought their first XJR-6 to a Group C race in Europe. I was driving a Porsche 962 then, and we had very complex Bosch electronic fuel-injection systems to eke

At Silverstone on 6th May 1986, Eddie Cheever
and Derek Warwick took a well deserved victory
in the 1000km race. It was something that
the Group C Jaguars were to make a habit of.
(Courtesy Graham Robson)

... we would race at only some 80 per cent of available
power, and there was this big green and white TWR Jaguar,
with its huge V12 engine, that would just go thundering by ...

JOHN FITZPATRICK

out the fuel allowance that we were given by the race organisers. Consequently, we would race at only some 80 per cent of available power, and there was this big green and white TWR Jaguar, with its huge V12 engine that would just go thundering by."

At Fuji, all the cars from Europe retired at the start of the race due to a cyclone hitting the track, but this did not stop the Nissan-engined March 85G driven by Hoshino, who simply hurtled off in the atrocious conditions, and, despite doing a full 360-degree spin, lapped the field before the flag was waved for his victory after just 62 laps.

Things looked up at Selangor, in Malaysia, where Jan Lammers, Mike Thackwell and John Nielsen finished second on the same lap as the winning works Porsche 956C driven by Jochen Mass and Jackie Ickx. Having amassed enough points, Derek Bell and Hans Stuck, (BEST), were declared joint World Endurance Champions for 1985.

Over the winter of 1985-86, TWR worked hard on developing the XJR-6 and the substitution of the single bag tank, instead of the previous three, coupled with getting rid of the previously needed extra pumps and filters, plus omitting the onboard jacking system, and further lightening of the bodywork, brought the weight down to 860kg. The engine size went up to 6.5 litres, and Allan Scott's work produced an engine that now developed 700 horsepower with 570lb-ft plus of torque from 5000 to 6750rpm. By the careful reduction of weight, the engines now weighed 235kg each, including the clutch, flywheel, engine management box, and wiring loom, but without the exhaust system. By comparison, a production Jaguar V12 weighed some 300kg.

One very important "tweak" that the XJR-6s received for 1986 was a fuel/lap meter within reach of the driver, mounted on top of the dashboard. This could be programmed for each circuit visited, showing the exact amount of fuel needed for each lap.

There were also two knobs on the dashboard, which read from 0 to 5. Fuel mixture was governed by one and ignition timing by the other. By adjusting these according to speed and conditions, the driver could keep to an exact amount of fuel required for each lap driven. This undoubtedly helped the drivers far more than the Porsche 962 method, which entailed a warning light coming on when the reserve supply needed to be

switched to, which told the driver that they needed to pit for fuel on the next lap.

To prevent the understeer, which had troubled the 1985 XJR-6s, Tony Southgate moved the start of the ground effect venturii forward from the rear of the carbon fibre tub to a point just beneath the driver's spine. So new monocoques were made, incorporating this modification. This moved the centre of pressure forward from 30 per cent at the front to 40 per cent. Le Mans regulations demanded a return to the old shape, so a filler panel was made and fitted to the old shape, which led on to venturii of decreased cross section. These new monocoques were also lighter by 10kg, as experience in building them had shown the makers where weight could be saved, whilst still retaining the necessary strength. The bodywork was also changed to a thinner gauge of composite carbon/Kevlar, plus an air intake on the engine compartment cover and larger brake cooling ducts were added.

All aspects of the car were looked at to make it lighter and more competitive; the gearbox had a magnesium casing and bell housing; for long distance races of six hours, the Salisbury differential was locked up to become, effectively, a spool. Nearly 60kg was saved, bringing the car's weight down to some 885kg, still some 35kg above the limit.

To accommodate the single tank in the cockpit bulkhead, the driver's seating position was moved forward by 2.5cm. Sponsorship, negotiated by Guy Edwards, was now provided by Silk Cut cigarettes and the cars looked very sleek and purposeful indeed in their new purple and white livery.

The season began with the Monza 1000km, and here the car of Eddie Cheever and Derek Warwick broke its driveshaft when well placed. The sister car of Jean-Louis Schlesser and Gianfranco Brancatelli ran out of fuel before the end of the race, something that happened to most of the rest of the entry.

TWR Jaguar scored its first World Championship victory in 1986, winning on home turf at the Silverstone 1000km race on May 5th, Derek Warwick and Eddie Cheever taking the victory, with the sister car delayed due to gear linkage problems, but still finishing seventh.

Eddie Cheever: "The first laps I did in the TWR Jaguar were at Snetterton in the wet. None of the doors were sealed, so I probably had a gallon of water in the car after the first three laps. The second test was a lot better,

Continued page 34

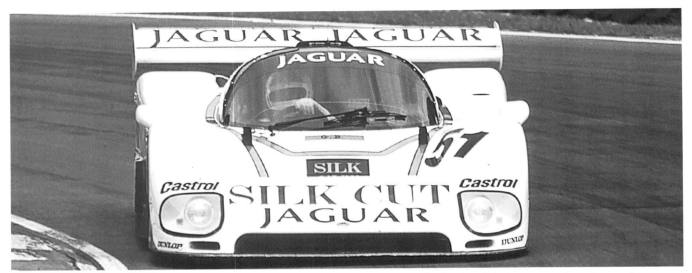

Derek Warwick and Eddie Cheever were two accomplished drivers at the height of their careers when they took Jaguar's first victory in Group C racing at Silverstone in May, 1986. They finished well ahead of the works Porsche 962s.
(Courtesy John S Allen)

Jean-Louis Schlesser and Gianfranco Brancatelli drove 186 at Silverstone in 1986. They finished in seventh place.
(Courtesy John S Allen)

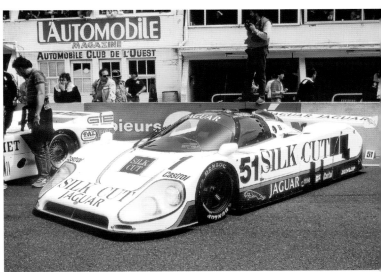

What a contrast. Chassis number 386 was the 'T' car at Silverstone in 1986, used for training/practice only, therefore leaving the race cars as fresh as possible for the 1000km. Here, it is posed next to a C Type Jaguar of the early 1950s, which had won Le Mans twice, in 1951 and 1953. (Courtesy John S Allen)

Eddie Cheever, Jean-Louis Schlesser and Derek Warwick drove chassis number 286 at Le Mans in June 1986. Sadly, they were forced into retirement when the suspension failed. (Courtesy John S Allen)

Waiting for its turn to go to the scrutineers is chassis number 186, in the paddock at Le Mans in 1986. Driven by Hurley Haywood, Hans Heyer and Brian Redman, it retired with fuel pump failure. (Courtesy John S Allen)

Rounding Mulsanne corner early in the Le Mans 24 hours of 1986 goes chassis number 186. Fuel pump failure saw it retire later on. (Courtesy John S Allen)

I loved the big V12 and Tony Southgate produced a car that created an enormous amount of downforce. A lot of fun to drive around tracks like Spa and Silverstone. A beast. During a GP, Senna stopped me once and asked me a bunch of pointed questions about the car: he wasn't a very chatty person so I remembered it."

Of course, the Le Mans 24 hours was THE race that TWR and Jaguar wanted to win above all else, but winning it at first try was perhaps a tad too ambitious. Nevertheless, at the April test day, TWR arrived with cars in three different configurations; one 'standard' car, set up for the usual 1000km races, but with its front splitter made smaller and its rear wing set down so that, although it was still above the rear deck, it was on a level with the top of the rear wheelarches.

The second car had smaller diffusers for less drag down the Mulsanne straight, and another had the full 'Longtail' Le Mans treatment with modifications to most of its bodywork. This car recorded 221mph down the Mulsanne straight whilst the car with the smaller diffusers ran 214mph. The 'standard' 1000km car could 'only' reach 190mph, but was almost as fast over a lap as the longtailed, 221mph XJR-6. Its problem was that it consumed 25 per cent more fuel and its driveshafts ran at an angle that portended driveshaft failure. The 'interim' car was a little quicker but also used more fuel than the longtail, and it was unstable down the Mulsanne straight.

So the longtail version was used for the race proper, and three were entered. They all retired, one running out of fuel, one when a driveshaft broke, and the third due to tyre failure. Despite these results, the cars had shown

Another shot of TWR-XJR-6 number 286 at Brands Hatch. (Courtesy John S Allen)

great speed, and were obviously going to be contenders for victory in the coming years.

The rest of the season saw a mixture of high placings, such as at the Norisring at the end of June where the two XJR-6s finished second and third, but no further victories. They suffered retirements caused by problems with wheel bearings, electrical gremlins and fuel pumps. Typical of this was the second race held on British soil, the 1000km race at Brands Hatch, held on July 20th. The Warwick/Schlesser car ran well but had to pit with blocked fuel filters, finally finishing in fourth place

The most embarrassing result was that at Jerez, in Spain on August 3rd, where there were three XJR-6s entered and they punted each other off at the first corner ... Derek Warwick dug himself out of the gravel trap into which he spun and made a heroic effort to finish third, with Jan Lammers.

The race at the Nürburgring on August 24th was a shambles, dreadful weather being the backdrop to a big multi car shunt after 22 laps, when Hans Stuck, the leader, never saw that the pace car had been called out and hit Jochen Mass, also driving a Porsche 962. The pair then hit other drivers, all this when Derek Warwick was lying third. When the race was restarted, Warwick took the lead but had to retire when the oil supply to the camshafts failed. This was caused by an oil pipe that had fractured whilst in transit.

It was this race that saw the first victory for the team that would become TWR Jaguar's main rival for the World Sports Car Championship in the coming years, Sauber. Peter Sauber's Swiss company had entered their Leo Ress designed C8, which was powered by a Heini Mader tuned Mercedes 5-litre 16-valve V8, fitted with twin turbochargers, which ran at a low pressure. 700

At Brands Hatch for the 1000km race of 1986, the new Silk Cut-sponsored TWR Jaguar XJR-6s made a great impression. Race number 51 was chassis number 286. Driven by Eddie Cheever and Gianfranco Brancatelli, it finished in sixth place overall. (Courtesy John S Allen)

1986 Brands Hatch: Derek Warwick and Jean-Louis Schlesser drove chassis number 386 to a fourth place finish. (Courtesy John S Allen)

Martin Brundle. One of THE star drivers for Tom Walkinshaw Racing. (Courtesy Graham Robson)

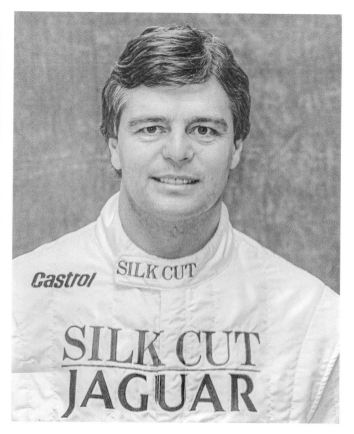

Derek Warwick. (Courtesy Jaguar)

horsepower was quoted at 6600rpm. The chassis was a conventional monocoque, mainly of bonded aluminium, clothed with Rudiger Faul designed bodywork of Kevlar reinforced glassfibre. At the Nürburgring, Mike Thackwell and Henri Pescarolo well deserved their victory in the atrocious conditions, Thackwell actually overtaking the recognised 'Rainmeister,' Hans Stuck, at one point

The race at Spa-Francorchamps on September 15th saw the most dramatic finish to any race that year, when Derek Warwick found himself catching the leader, Thierry Boutsen, on the last lap when the leading Porsche began running out of fuel. Warwick squeezed by at the last corner, only for his car to run out of fuel and Boutsen's engine to suddenly burst into life with its last dregs, beating Warwick to the line by 0.8 of a second.

For TWR, the most interesting part of this race had been that Allan Scott had built an engine of 6829cc capacity, by using an increased stroke of 82mm. Scott

had learned that, above 6800rpm, fuel efficiency had decreased, mainly due to frictional losses. With this engine installed in his XJR-6, Eddie Cheever set a lap time of 2:07.30: as fast as the works Porsches. With his 'usual' 6.5-litre engine installed, Eddie Cheever was 0.5 seconds slower.

One week later, at the Nürburgring for the second time, Eddie Cheever achieved victory for TWR Jaguar, his XJR-6 using the same 6829cc engine that had been tried in testing at Spa. The race was called a 'Supercup,' and was only 177km. In qualifying, Hans Stuck took pole with Klaus Ludwig alongside, then came Eddie Cheever, driving solo, Bruno Giacomelli in a privately entered Lancia, and then Bob Wollek.

There were two heat races on the Saturday of seven laps each. Klaus Ludwig won the first heat with Eddie Cheever second. Stuck won the second heat, with Oscar Larrauri second, Bob Wollek third, and Eddie Cheever fourth.

*Jan Lammers. The smiling Dutchman began racing
for TWR in 1985, and was still with the team in 1990.
(Courtesy Graham Robson)*

*John Nielsen: Although born in Denmark, John Lived in
Germany. After 1987 he did most of his racing in IMSA in the
USA for TWR. (Courtesy Graham Robson)*

Eddie Cheever was third for the first part of the race, with Stuck and Wollek ahead of him, but moved into second place when the boost control on the Richard Lloyd Racing 962 failed. The result was in doubt until the last corner, where the works Porsche of 'Stuckie' stuttered with fuel starvation and Eddie Cheever took the win by just over half a second.

Right up to the last race, held at Fuji in Japan, Jaguar was in with a chance of winning the World Championship. To win, Eddie Cheever and Derek Warwick's car had to finish no lower than second, with the Porsche factory Rothmans team out of the points. It

was a tall order and at the finish, Cheever and Warwick, who had been delayed by small electrical faults, finished third. Although disappointed at the result, TWR and Jaguar could see that they were on the right track.

At the end of the season, Gianfranco Brancatelli and Jean-Louis Schlesser left the team. Brancatelli went back to saloon car racing but Jean-Louis Schlesser went to Sauber-Mercedes and became World Sports car Champion in 1988 and 1990. Of course, he was able to be debriefed by Mercedes about how TWR governed their fuel useage, which cannot have hurt their chances in the coming years.

Constructor Tom Walkinshaw Racing, 1 Station Field Industrial Estate, Kidlington, Oxford, England

Chassis fabricator Advanced Composite Technology Ltd., Composites House, Adams Close, Heanor Gate Industrial Estate, Heanor, Derbyshire, DE7 7SW

Chassis Carbon fibre and kevlar monocoque with steel tube supports for engine, designed by Tony Southgate. Single front located Serck water radiator. Twin side mounted Serck oil radiators. Premier fuels Systems Ltd., 95-litre (Group C) fuel tank in mid position. 12-litre oil tank in front left-hand side of engine bay

Body Kevlar, carbon fibre and GRP. Wing and full ground effect underbody in carbon fibre. Underside with regulation flat surfaces and air-ducts as permitted by the regulations.

Aerodynamics include enclosed rear wheels, except on Le Mans cars, which also have less ground effect and body/wing modifications demanded by that circuit.

Engine (Group C) TWR Jaguar 60-degree V12 (Allan Scott) Unblown, liquid cooled
92.0 x 78.0mm/6.2 litres (1985)
94.0 x 78.0mm/6537cc (1986)
94.0 x 82mm/6829cc (Spa, 1986)
Aluminium block and heads
Stressed chassis member
Wet cast iron liners
Seven plain main bearings
Nitrided EN40B steel crankshaft with Holset harmonic damper
Steel con rods
Cosworth alloy pistons. Goetze rings
SOHC – single duplex chain driven
Two titanium valves/cylinder, one plug (Champion)
Zytek engine management and telemetry
Bosch injection, Lucas ignition
AP 7.25in 3-plate clutch
Compression ratio 11.8:1
736bhp at 7000rpm, with peak torque at 593ft-lb/6850rpm. Maximum rpm 7600

(6.5-litre 1986 engines)
Weight 235kg including clutch

Suspension (front) Wide-base fabricated wishbones actuating pushrods to coil/damper units mounted horizontally at centre-line of the car. Magnesium alloy hub carriers.

Suspension (rear) Magnesium alloy uprights and steel coils. Shock absorbers and brake discs housed within wheel hubs to allow maximum venturi width.

AP four-pot calipers and 13in cast iron brake discs. Dymag 19in rims Koni shocks front, Bilstein rear.

Gearbox March/TWR 5 speed, with straight cut gears.

General Cockpit electrically adjustable rear-view mirrors. Four Oscar/Cibie headlamps. MRTC radio. Lifeline fire system. Pipercross air filters. Goodridge flexible piping and unions.

Dimensions Wheelbase – 2710mm
Length – 4820mm.
Width – 2020mm
Height – 1031mm.
Front track – 1500mm
Rear track – 1450mm
Weight 885kg (Group C)

XJR6 – 185 **Green, Jaguar**

1985:
03/08: Mosport 1000km: M Brundle/M Thackwell, #51; DNF (wheel bearing)
01/09: Spa-Francorchamps: M Brundle/M Thackwell, #51; 5th
22/09: Brands Hatch 1000km: A Jones/JL Schlesser, # 51; DNF (engine)
06/10: Fuji 1000km: M Thackwell/J Nielsen, #51; DNS (weather)
09/12: Selangor: M Thackwell/J Nielsen/J Lammers, #51; 2nd

1986:
03-06: Tests at Estoril, Portugal
In TWR Collection
Sold to Henry Pearman, for a customer

Rebuilt and in private UK-based collection

XJR-6 – 285   Green / Jaguar

1985:
03/08: Mosport 1000km: JL Schlesser/Brundle/Thackwell, #52; 3rd
01/09: Spa-Francorchamps: JL Schlesser/Heyer, #52; DNF (handling)
22/09: Brands Hatch 1000km: Lammers/Heyer, #52; DNF (engine)
06/10: Fuji 1000km: H Heyer/S Soper #52; DNS (weather)
09/12: Selangor: J Lammers/Brancatelli, #52; DNF (tyre)

1986:
03-06: Tested at Estoril, Portugal
Sold in auction at Goodwood Festival of Speed
Sold to David Coplowe
STP0

XJR-6 – 385   Purple/White, the first Silk Cut car

1986:
20/04: Monza-T car
05/05: Silverstone-T-car
31/05-1/06: Le Mans 24 hours: G Brancatelli/W Percy/H Hahne /H Haywood, #53; DNF (driveshaft)
Repaired, and placed in TWR's museum

1989:
Sold to Tony Kember

1990:
Track tested, *Jaguar Quarterly*, Issue 4, Vol 2, Summer 1990

1991:
Bought back by TWR

2000:
STP0

XJR-6 – 186

1986:
20/04: Monza Supersprint: G Brancatelli /JL Schlesser, #52; DNF (fuel)
05/05: Silverstone 1000km: JL Schlesser/G Brancatelli, #52; 7th
31/05-1/06: Le Mans 24 hours: H Heyer/H Haywood/B Redman, #52; DNF (fuel pressure)
29/06: Norisring Supersprint: D Warwick, #52; 3rd
20/07: Brands Hatch 1000km: JL Schlesser/D Warwick #52; T-Car, DNS
03/08: Jerez Supersprint: G Brancatelli/JL Schlesser, #53; DNF (driveshaft)
24/08 Nürburgring 1000km: G Brancatelli/ J Lammers/D Warwick, #53; DNF (engine)
14/09 Spa-Francochamps 1000km: E Cheever/J Lammers/JL Schlesser/D Warwick, #51T; T car only
21/09 Norisring: E Cheever, #51; 1st (non championship race)
October: Upgraded to Le Mans specification, as XJR-8LM

See 1987 results

XJR-6 – 286

1986:
Silk-Cut sponsored
20/04: Monza Supersprint: E Cheever/D Warwick, #51; DNF (driveshaft)
05/05: Silverstone 1000km: E Cheever/D Warwick, #51; 1st
31/5-1/06: Le Mans 24 hours: E Cheever/D Warwick/JL Schlesser, #51; DNF (suspension)
29/06: Norisring Supersprint: E Cheever, #51; 2nd
20/07: Brands Hatch 1000km: E Cheever/D Warwick/ Brancatelli, #51; 6th
03/08: Jerez Supersprint: E Cheever/Brundle, #51; DNF (driveshaft)
24/08: Nürburgring 1000km: E Cheever/Schlesser/Heyer, #51; DNF (driveshaft)
15/09: Spa-Francorchamps 1000km: E Cheever/JL Schlesser, #51; 5th

06/10: Fuji 1000km: E Cheever/D Warwick, #51; 3rd
October: Upgraded to Le Mans specification, as XJR-8LM

See 1987 results

XJR-6 – 386

1986:
29/06: Norisring: JL Schlesser, #53; 17th
20/07: Brands Hatch 1000km: D Warwick/JL Schlesser, #53; 4th

03/08: Jerez Supersprint: D Warwick/J Lammers, #52; 3rd
24/08: Nürburgring 1000km: D Warwick/J Lammers, #52; DNR (Warwick crashed in qualifying)
15/09: Spa-Francorchamps 1000km: D Warwick/J Lammers, #52; 2nd
06/10: Fuji 1000km: G Brancatelli/J Lammers/JL Schlesser, #52; 17th

See next chapter for 1987 results

> I loved the big V12 and Tony Southgate produced a car that created an enormous amount of downforce. A lot of fun to drive around tracks like Spa and Silverstone. A beast.

EDDIE CHEEVER

Chapter 4

XJR-8 1987

For 1987, development continued at a frantic pace at TWRs base at Kidlington. The 'standard' 1000km race car had no less than sixty-four modifications compared to the preceding XJR-6 and was now known as the XJR-8.

As we have seen, the XJR-7 appellation had already been used by the Group 44 team in America.

Allan Scott, in charge of the engines at TWR's Kidlington base, now produced a '7-litre' variant of the

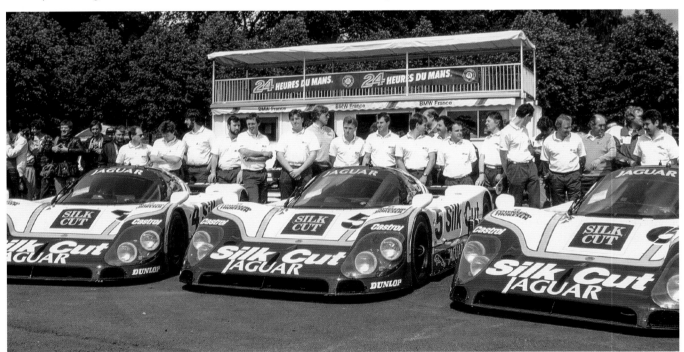

All lined up for the official photo before the start of the Le Mans 24-hour race in 1987. Only the car on the left, number 4, would see the end of the race in fifth place, driven by Raul Boesel, Eddie Cheever and Jan Lammers. Race number five had its engine fail and a tyre blowout at full speed, with Win Percy driving, wrecked car #5. Due to the car's inherent strength, Win Percy was able to walk away unhurt. (Courtesy John S Allen)

An overhead photo of one of the TWR Jaguars being refueled in the pits. (Courtesy Graham Robson)

big V12. With a bore and stroke of 94mm x 84mm, it actually displaced 6995cc, and its advantage was in the increased torque it generated. Although its maximum horsepower was only some 15-20 more than the previous 6.5-litre engine employed, it produced an extra 45 horsepower at less than peak revs, which helped mileage and drivability both.

For Le Mans in particular, the XJR-8LM had its engine mounted at an angle so that it was higher at the back, in order to reduce the angle of the drive shafts; the starter motor was made easier to change, and even the tyre temperature sensors were now mounted in the wheelarches, the easier to spot the increasing temperature of a deflating tyre. These tyre carcasses, incidentally, were now of a new, Kevlar construction.

There were ten races in the World Championship that year and the TWR Jaguars won seven of them; the two

that eluded the team were Le Mans and the Norisring sprint.

At the opening race at Jarama, Spain, the two XJR-8s entered were on the front row. At the finish, Jan Lammers and John Watson were the winners, the works Porsche of Derek Bell and Hans Stuck second, and the XJR-8 of Eddie Cheever and Raol Boesel (a new signing) third.

It was Cheever and Boesel's turn to win at the next race, held just a week later at Jerez. On this very bumpy track, the sister car retired with a broken driveshaft, and Porsche 962s were second and third.

Just two weeks later, it was Monza in sunny Italy, and TWR Jaguar won yet again, this time with Jan Lammers and John Watson taking the honors. This even though Lammers had spun just six laps in, whilst Raul Boesel in the other car spun six laps from the finish, into a gravel trap ...

Seated on the surviving XJR-8 (chassis number 387) prior to the race at Le Mans are, from left to right, Raul Boesel, Jan Lammers and John Watson. (Courtesy John S Allen)

At Silverstone on May 10th, 23,000 people watched TWR Jaguar take a one-two finish, Raul Boesel and Eddie Cheever winning handily with John Watson and Jan Lammers finishing second, well clear of the works run Rothmans Porsche 962 of Derek Bell and Hans Stuck. At last, Porsche seemed to realise that it was on the back foot where Group C racing was concerned.

It was after this race, and before the Le Mans 24 hours, that the Jaguar factory finally announced that TWR would, in future, be the company that they would be backing. John Egan had carefully weighed up the needs of Jaguar's main market, America, and, even bearing in mind the brand loyalty that the Group 44 Jaguars engendered, he could clearly see that the TWR cars were superior in speed and reliability to the Lee Dykstra-designed XJR-7.

Eddie Cheever: "Driving for Tom was a great experience. He was extremely focused on the cars. He took great pride in making sure the car got better race to race. His favourite component was obviously the engine. I don't recall any race as being the hardest, but beating Porsche, Mercedes and my teammates always required hundred per cent effort."

Allan Scott and Roger Silman, the team manager of TWR, were sent by Tom Walkinshaw to the Group 44 headquarters in Virginia. As both men were needed back in Kidlington as quickly as possible, given the looming race at Le Mans, they flew Concorde there and back, the whole journey taking just 23 hours. The overall impression that they reported back to Tom Walkinshaw was that the Group 44 shop was in the middle of a very

Gridded in fifth and sixth, two of the XJR-8s move off for the rolling start at Le Mans in 1987. Ahead is one of the works Rothmans Porsche 962s, and car number 62 is one of those that would present Jaguar with its greatest challenge in the years to come: the Sauber, this one a C8. (Courtesy John S Allen)

expensive area, and some employees were having to drive 50 miles to work, as low or even 'reasonably' priced housing was unavailable.

At Le Mans, Win Percy had a huge accident on the Mulsanne straight due to a deflating tyre, but emerged unhurt. A second car had a cracked cylinder head and the third one was delayed by gearbox problems: Stuck, Holbert and Bell won again for Porsche.

Eddie Cheever: "What I regret the most was leading Le Mans with just a few hours to go and having mechanical failures. To this day it bothers me. Heartbreaking.

"When I accepted an offer from Ganassi to race in IndyCar I had just concluded a great extension of my contract with Tom. When I look back at the Jaguar Le

Mans success it is somewhat frustrating not having been part of a TWR Le Mans winning effort ..."

At the Norisring on June 28th, one XJR-8 had its differential fail, whilst the other had engine problems.

Brands Hatch saw another TWR Jaguar victory on July 26th, this time by Raul Boesel, joined by John Nielsen. Both the TWR-run cars had been on the front row, but Jan Lammers and John Watson had problems with a faulty wheel bearing that dropped them to third at the finish.

The Teams' Championship was won by TWR Jaguar at the next race, held at the Nürburgring on August 30th. Sadly, the XJR-8 of Jan Lammers/John Watson was an early retirement but the car driven by Raul Boesel, and

Seen here at Mulsanne corner on the afternoon of the first few hours is chassis number 286, the car that was later very badly damaged in a high speed crash. (Courtesy John S Allen)

At Brands Hatch on the 26th July, 1987, this XJR-8 (chassis number 287) won outright, driven by Raul Boesel and John Nielsen. (Courtesy John S Allen)

Eddie Cheever won outright, heading home a phalanx of Porsche 962s in the next seven places.

The 1000km race held at Spa-Francorchamps was next, and this race saw another TWR Jaguar one-two, Raul Boesel being joined by Johnny Dumfries and Martin Brundle to take the win, with Jan Lammers and John Watson second. Eddie Cheever and John Nielsen in another XJR-8 were fourth, narrowly failing to catch the Brun entered Porsche 962 of Oscar Larrauri and Jochen Mass. It was this race and result that saw Raul Boesel crowned as the Drivers' Champion in the FIA World Sports Prototype Championship, to give it its full title.

It was a slam dunk, leaving only the race at Mount Fuji in Japan on September 27th to end the season, and here again, it was a TWR Jaguar one-two, Jan Lammers and John Watson this time taking the honors, with Raul Boesel and Johnny Dumfries finishing second on the same lap as the winners.

At the end of the season, Raul Boesel of Brazil had been crowned Drivers' Champion and TWR Jaguar had won the manufacturers' crown, the World Sportscars Championship.

The view that most competitors saw of the TWR Jaguar XJR-8s during 1987. (Courtesy John S Allen)

John Nielsen at Daytona in late 1987, at the test of the TWR Jaguar XJR-9. (Courtesy Lee Self)

During the summer of 1987, Tom Walkinshaw appointed Tony Dowe as his manager for the TWR racing effort in America, and a shop was located and purchased in Valparaiso, Indiana, near Indianapolis, as this was the centre of racing in America and there were a lot of machine shops in the area that could produce the necessary parts for making and maintaining racecars.

In September, an XJR-9, as the American TWR-entered Jaguars were known, was sent to Valparaiso and prepared to IMSA specification. It went to Daytona to test at the end of October, then to Texas for more testing in November, and then to the super speedway at Talladega, in January 1988, before finally going to Daytona to test for the 24-hour race there.

For racing in IMSA, the XJR-9s had larger ground effect venturii than were allowed in Europe by Group C rules. They also had to run a smaller V12 engine of 6 litres, and the cars had to be ballasted to IMSA's minimum weight regulation by having a 150lb plate made of aluminium, 6mm thick, bolted to the floor. A bigger, 120-litre fuel tank than was allowed in Group C was fitted, but the car was forced to have smaller 17in diameter wheels instead of its Group C 18in diameter ones.

TWR came to Daytona to test in December 1987, where these four photos were taken. The car used was probably chassis number 188. (Courtesy Lee Self)

When I look back at the Jaguar Le Mans success it is somewhat frustrating not having been part of a TWR Le Mans-winning effort ...

EDDIE CHEEVER

186

1987:
Uprated to XJR-8 spec, 186 became TWR-J12C-186
10/05: Silverstone 1000km: M Brundle/J Nielsen, #6; DNF (engine)
13-14/06: Le Mans: M Brundle/J Nielsen/H Hahne, #6; DNF (engine)

1987:
Tested at Paul Ricard. Uprated to XJR-9LM spec, then to XJR-9LM spec

286

1987:
13-14/06: Le Mans 24 hours: J Lammers/W Percy/J Watson, #5; DNF (accident)

1989:
Rebuilt, using new tub and sold to a collector in Japan.

386

1987:
22/03: Jarama: # 4T; used as T car by all the drivers
29/03: Jerez: # 4T; used as T car by all the drivers
12/04: Monza: # 4T; used as T car by all the drivers
10/05: Silverstone: # 4T; used as T car by all the drivers
Show car

1988
Renumbered to 188

1991:
Renumbered to 991
22-23/06: Le Mans 24 hours: T Fabi/B Wollek/K Acheson, #34; 3rd

XJR-8 Group C 1987

Essentially the same basic monocoque as XJR-6. Some of the old chassis were in fact renumbered as new cars, but with numerous detail changes and a 7.0-litre engine. First win at debut race – Jarama 360km, 22nd March 1987 driven by Lammers and Watson. Eight WSPC wins out of ten starts during 1987. Five wins by Raul Boesel, who became World Drivers' Champion. TWR Jaguar World Teams' Champion. Weight 850kg.

XJR-8 – 187

1987:
22/03: Jarama: J Lammers/J Watson, #5: 1st
29/03: Jerez: J Lammers/J Watson, #5: DNF (driveshaft)
12/04: Monza: J Lammers/J Watson, #5: 1st
10/05: Silverstone: J Lammers/J Watson, #5: 2nd
28/06: Norisring: J Lammers/J Watson, #5; DNF (gearbox)
26/07: Brands Hatch: J Lammers/J Watson, #5: 3rd
30/08: Nürburgring: J Lammers/J Watson, #5: DNF (engine)
13/09: Spa: J Lammers/J Watson, #5: 2nd.
27/09: Fuji: J Lammers/J Watson, #5: 1st

Upgraded to XJR-9, see 1988 results

XJR-8 – 287

1987:
22/03: Jarama: E Cheever/R Boesel, #4; 3rd
29/03: Jerez: E Cheever/R Boesel, #4; 1st
12/04: Monza: J Nielsen/R Boesel, #4; DNF (spun off whilst leading)
10/05: Silverstone: E Cheever/R Boesel, #4; 1st
28/06: Norisring: E Cheever/R Boesel, #4; 4th
26/07:Brands Hatch: J Nielsen/R Boesel, #4; 1st
30/08: Nürburgring: E Cheever/R Boesel, #4; 1st
13/09: Spa: E Cheever/J Nielsen, #4; 4th
27/09: Fuji: R Boesel/J Dumfries, #4; 2nd

Upgraded to XJR-9 specification, see 1988 results

XJR-8 – 387

1987:
13-14/06: Le Mans: E Cheever/R Boesel/J Lammers, #4; 5th
28/06: Norisring test car; DNS
05/07: Hockenheim: R Boesel, # 4: 3rd non championship race
26/07: Brands Hatch: # 4T; T car only
30/08: Nürburgring: # 4 T; T car only
13/09: Spa 1000km: M Brundle/J Dumfries/R Boesel, #4 # 6; 1st

1989:
Restored at TWR, and sold to a European collector

Chapter 5

XJR-9 1988

1988 was the year that TWR Jaguar entered the IMSA series in America, and with the team led by ex-Englishman Tony Dowe, it won first time out at the Daytona 24 hours. John Nielsen, Raul Boesel and Jan Lammers took the victory, with the Porsche 962 of Bob Wollek, Mauro Baldi and Brian Redman taking second place, and the sister XJR-9 of Eddie Cheever, Johnny Dumfries and John Watson in third.

For TWR, the race had been preceded by extensive testing, particularly where the new 6.0-litre engine was concerned. Tom Walkinshaw had blithely assumed that his cars would be allowed to use the 7.0-litre engine that they had used in Europe. The new rules by IMSA, probably lobbied for by its Porsche 962 customers, of

which there were many, came just four months before the Daytona 24 hours, and were a rude surprise, but Allan Scott, head of the engine department at Kidlington, was up to the challenge he was faced with.

Using a new crankshaft, the 7.0-litre engine's stroke was shortened from 84mm to 72mm, and Farndon Engineering produced it from EN40B steel forgings. Cosworth Engineering built new pistons giving 13.5:1 compression ratio. The inlet tracts now were 2mm smaller in diameter, which would improve the mid-range torque of the engine. This design allowed TWR to continue using the original 7.0-litre size cylinder liners, conrods, camshafts, valve gear, block, sump, oil system and ancillaries which were by now well proven. Bosch

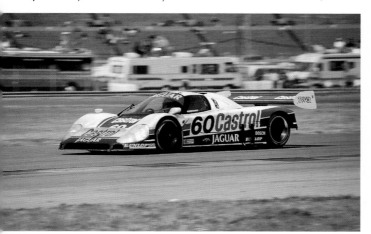
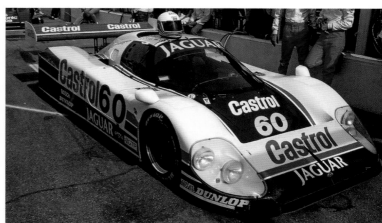

The winning TWR Jaguar XJR-9D of Martin Brundle, Raul Boesel, John Nelson and Jan Lammers at the Daytona 24 hours in 1988.
(Courtesy Lee Self)

Eddie Cheever during the 1988 Daytona 24 hours. Together with Johnny Dumfries and John Watson, their car, chassis number 188, finished in third place. (Courtesy Lee Self)

The end of January 1988, and the XJR-9 of Davy Jones, Jan Lammers and Danny Sullivan sweeps through the infield at Daytona. Their engine failed, but the other two XJR-9s entered were first and third. (Courtesy Graham Robson)

Front and rear views of the two XJR-9Ds entered for the Sebring 12-hour race of 1988 being prepared.(Courtesy Lee Self)

sparkplugs replaced the previous ones supplied by Champion, and immediately this new engine produced 680 horsepower, before the design of the exhaust system had been finalised. The first engine was sent to the new TWR base at Valparaiso in December, allowing plenty of time for its installation in the car to be used in testing.

Eddie Cheever about Daytona: "The banking is really for cars racing on the oval. On the Daytona 24-hour track you can stay full throttle in the banking even when the track is wet. So the banking wasn't really an issue.

"I think we had an engine problem in that race which was very disappointing because I had John Watson as a teamate. I enjoyed driving with him and I would have liked to share a Daytona 24-hour win with him."

At the second race, held on the street circuit at Miami, John Nielsen and Martin Brundle lost out to the winning Porsche 962 of Price Cobb and James Weaver by just four thousandth of a second but the TWR Jaguars were well beaten in the Sebring 12-hour race, the sole

surviving XJR-9 finishing seventh and being beaten by six Porsche 962s and even a solitary 'Chevrolet Corvette' GTP car, which in reality was a Lola T711.

The two TWR Jaguars ready to go out at Sebring. (Courtesy Lee Self)

Right and opposite: This was the only TWR Jaguar XJR-9D number 61, 388, that finished the 1988 Sebring 12 hours. Driven by Jan Lammers, Davy Jones, Danny Sullivan and John Nielsen, it was running well until a broken input shaft of the gearbox forced a 42-minute repair, which relegated it to seventh place at the finish. Its sister car, chassis number 288, driven by Martin Brundle, Raul Boesel and John Nielsen, went out when the engine failed. (Courtesy Lee Self)

Jaguar lost no opportunity to use TWR's success in advertising its cars. (Courtesy IMSA Yearbook)

TWR Jaguar in England had much to look forward to as 1988 arrived. Having vanquished Porsche in the European Championship, it was not expecting the sort of opposition it faced from Peter Sauber's Mercedes engine-equipped Group C cars, and was surprised to be beaten at the first race at Jerez by the Swiss team, which now had official Mercedes backing. For the rest of the season the Sauber-Mercedes C9 gave the TWR Jaguar XJR-9s, as they were now called, a hard time.

Despite this new opposition, and the seeming hordes of private teams still running the now venerable Porsche 962, TWR Jaguar won the race it really wanted, the Le Mans 24 hours, and it won the Constructor's and Driver's Championships as well.

As mentioned, the season started at Jerez, Spain with an 800km race, and here, the singleton Sauber C9 of Jochen Mass, Mauro Baldi and Jean-Louis Schlesser claimed pole position by some two seconds over the best of the three TWR Jaguar XKR-9s that took the start. Jochen Mass, in an interview with the author, said: "You know, I would say that the TWR Jaguars had the upper edge on us aerodynamically at the start of 1988. I believe that we had the better engines but they had their problems as well as us."

Straight away, the cars from Kidlington led and looked in control, at one-third distance being 1-2-3 with the Sauber in fourth place. But then on lap 83, Andy Wallace had to pit to clear a blocked radiator inlet and two laps later, the car driven by Jan Lammers had its gearbox stick in fifth gear.

Although the Sauber was now in second place, this changed when Eddie Cheever, taking over from Martin Brundle, suddenly found that he could not select fourth or fifth gear. He retired on lap 139, out of 190 and the

The main opposition to TWR Jaguar in 1988. The Porsche 962 may have been beaten, but this new Sauber-Mercedes threat looked daunting ... (Courtesy LAT)

Sauber took the lead, only troubled by the XJR-9 of John Nielsen, John Watson and Andy Wallace, who were never able to get within striking distance of the black Sauber, due to their earlier forced pitstop. As usual, the leading pair were chased home by the four privateer Porsches of Joest (two cars), Richard Lloyd Racing and Brun. Gordon Spice and Ray Bellm's new Spice was the first C2 car to finish.

Eddie Cheever: "Both Raul (Boesel) and Martin (Brundle) won the championship as my teammates. I was racing in F1 and the calendars were not syncing very well.

"When we didn't have mechanical issues or driver errors we were the strongest team. I never considered the Sauber superior to our effort. I learn with TWR what it meant to start the race with the best equipment."

TWR Jaguar avenged this defeat the following weekend at the circuit of Jerez, this time in a 360km sprint race. Although the Sauber took pole, it was only by 0.6 of a second. The critical part of this race was dictated by the tyres, the TWR Jaguars having to make only one stop on their Kevlar-sheathed Dunlops, as compared with the Sauber needing two stops to change worn Michelins. Jochen Mass again: "Michelin are a great company but we had problems with their tyres at that time. Their tyres' sidewalls weren't strong enough to take the loadings that the Sauber-Mercedes put through them with its downforce, and they went off quite quickly. Michelin wanted Sauber to design a new car that would not have as much downforce as we already had, but of course, that would have taken us down the wrong road. Later on, we did win Le Mans with them, so they weren't that bad! But when we went to Goodyears, they were much better, stiffer tyres."

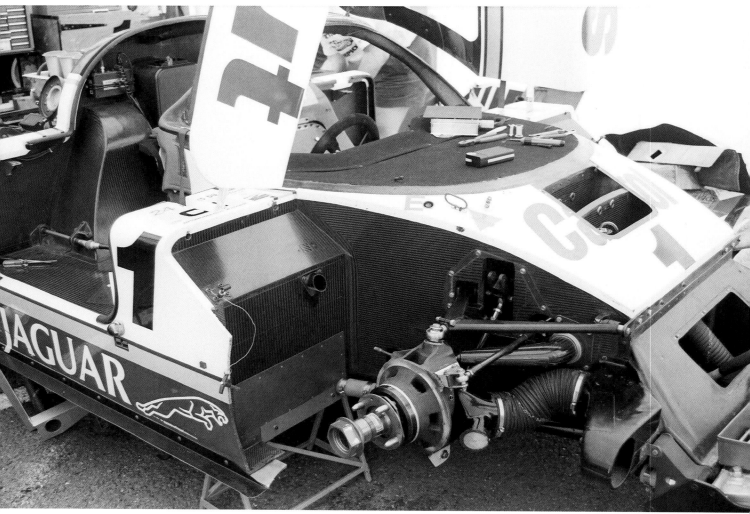

The front suspension of the Jaguar XJR-9 in 1988.

The race ended with Eddie Cheever and Martin Brundle the winners; the Sauber of Schlesser and Baldi second, after Dumfries had an 'off' into a gravel trap, and John Nielsen and John Watson third. Once again, the winning C2 car was the Spice of Ray Bellm and Gordon Spice.

On April 24th, the Monza 1000km race was held on the old fast circuit near to Milan. This year saw a problem with fuel supply. The organisers could supply only 97 RON fuel, whereas FISA specified a minimum of 98.7. The organisers stated that they could not provide the necessary fuel, so the teams banded together and bought a tanker-full from Germany. When that arrived

at the circuit, the organisers allowed it in but then confiscated it. Faced with the threat of a total boycott, the organisers released the truck to the teams and it became the official fuel of the meeting.

As Monza is a fast track, so the turbocharged Porsches come into their own, and the Brun and Joest-entered 962s qualified second and third behind the Sauber, ahead of the Jaguars. When it came time for the race to start, the three German cars were off like a shot, with the Jaguars biding their time. By the time the Mercedes and Porsche teams realised their mistake – that they were using too much fuel to finish – the Jaguars were

The unclothed rear of an XJR-9 in 1988. The rear suspension can be clearly seen, hanging from the crossbeam mounted on the gearbox, which enabled very large venture to be fitted for maximum ground effect. (Courtesy John S Allen)

on them as they slowed. Martin Brundle and Eddie Cheever won, with the Sauber second and Porsche 962s in the next four places. The Sauber had spun and had been collected by Jan Lammers, necessitating Lammers' retirement but the Sauber only suffered a bent wheelrim. Dumfries did his usual and spun into a gravel trap.

Silverstone on May 8th saw a crowd of 35,000 show up in the hopes of watching the TWR Jaguars win yet again, and they were not disappointed. For the first time, the Sauber team fielded two entries, one of the older C9-87/88 chassis and one brand new C9-88. Qualifying saw

Jean-Louis Schlesser gain a commanding pole position, some 1.5 seconds faster than the Brundle/Cheever XJR-9.

At the start of the race, Eddie Cheever thrilled the crowds with some close racing between him and the two Saubers but when Martin Brundle took over, he swiftly drew out a 30 second lead as the Sauber drivers realised that they had to keep their eyes on the fuel gauge to make the finish. Lammers and Dumfries suffered the indignity of running out of fuel five laps from the end, despite the readout telling the Earl of Dumfries that he had 9 litres of fuel left, which it obviously did not have.

The fans expect ... 1988 at Le Mans, and obviously these fans understand that it's the TWR team from Kidlington, near to Banbury, that's running the show ... (Courtesy John S Allen)

And then it was Le Mans time ... TWR Jaguar entered no less than five cars, and three of them saw the chequered flag on Sunday afternoon, one of them being the winning car. But before that, what was shaping up to be a titanic battle between the Jaguars and the Saubers came to naught. In practice on the Wednesday, Klaus Niedzwiedz was exiting the Mulsanne kink (this was in the days before the two chicanes, which appeared in 1990) at somewhere over 230mph, when his rear nearside Michelin exploded, destroying much of the rear bodywork. By skilful driving, and some luck, he kept the

The number 3 car at Le Mans was chassis number 287, an XJR-9LM. Driven by Raul Boesel, John Watson and Henri Pescarolo, it retired with transmission problems. (Courtesy John S Allen)

Sauber off the barriers and made his way slowly to the pits. No solution to the problem could be found and so on the Friday morning, Peter Sauber withdrew the team from the race. Scratch one competitor.

There remained one ominous competitor, that could not be discounted. Fitted with liquid-cooled engines with their own electronic wastegate control and the latest Bosch Motronic 1.7 engine management, the three works-entered, Shell-sponsored Porsche 962s were a very real threat. They duly took pole position, TWR Jaguar opting to concentrate on race setup instead. Indeed Hans Stuck set an incredible time in practice of 3:15.64, which was out of reach of the XJR-9s, who had to content themselves with fourth, Brundle/Nielsen) and sixth (Lammers/Wallace/Dumfries) as their best two places.

The Porsches led at the start, but by the sixth lap Jan Lammers was ahead, to great roars of approval from the many British spectators. For three hours, the TWR Jaguar XJR-9 led until hit in the rear by Pareja's 962. The 962 Porsche of Bob Wollek, Sarel van der Merwe and Vern Schuppan challenged the Jaguar, but the turbocharged engine of the 962 blew after 12 hours.

Jan Lammers drove the final stint, and, despite the works 962 of Derek Bell/Hans Stuck and Klaus Ludwig closing on him, comfortably won the race. Two other American-driven XJR-9s finished in fourth and 16th places, but two XJR-9s retired, one with a blown head gasket and one with a broken gearbox.

Jan Lammers' co-drivers had been John Nielsen and Andy Wallace. When asked about his time driving for TWR Jaguar, Andy Wallace said: "I had won the Formula 3 Championship in 1986, and the final race was at Macau, a big occasion in those days. Going into the last lap, Jan Lammers was ahead of me and I tried to overtake him at the end of the main straight. He left his braking so late that the rear tyres locked up and he

The winning car at speed. Driven by Jan Lammers, Johnny Dumfries and Andy Wallace, it beat the works Porsche 962 of Derek Bell and Hans Stuck into second place. (Courtesy John S Allen)

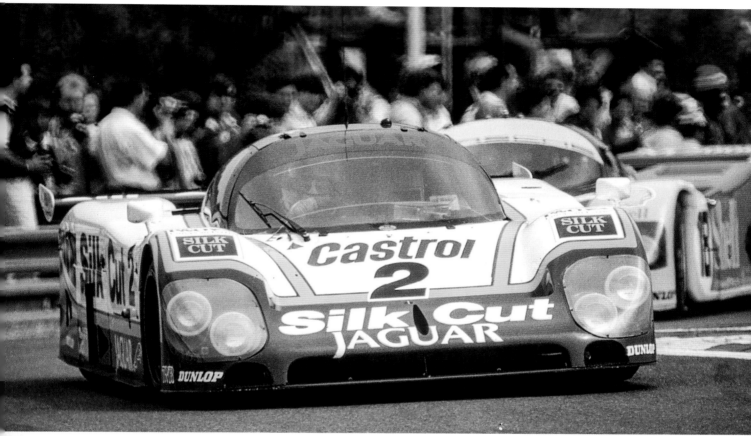

The winning Jaguar being pursued by the second placed Shell-sponsored works Porsche 962C of Hans Stuck and Derek Bell. (Courtesy John S Allen)

started to spin. I saw my opportunity and dived for the inside of the corner and overtook Jan, in the process half clipping his wheels and straightening him up! He chased me round for the rest of the lap and, after I had won the race, came over to thank me for straightening him up as, without that he said, he would have gone into the wall.

"Jan recommended me to TWR, and I shall be eternally grateful to him for that. I went for a test at Paul Ricard with TWR and got the drive. Sometimes you need a bit of luck ...

"When we went to Le Mans in 1988, both Jan and Johnny Dumfries helped me a lot with learning to drive to the Group C formula of only having so much fuel to work with to get to the end of the race."

> "I think we V-maxed at about 240mph ... It's all fine until it's not!

MARTIN BRUNDLE

◀ *Andy Wallace started racing with TWR in 1988, and swiftly proved to be one of the very best. (Courtesy Graham Robson)*

▶ *Victory! (Courtesy John S Allen)*

▼ *The winning Jaguar, race number 2, being driven by Jan Lammers, crosses the start finish line at Le Mans in 1988. Behind it is the #22 car, driven by Derek Daly, Kevin Coogan and Larry Perkins, whilst behind that is car #21, driven by Danny Sullivan, Davy Jones and Price Cobb. (Courtesy Graham Robson)*

▼ *The winning XJR-9LM (chassis number 488), on display in 1988. (Courtesy John S Allen)*

◄ The winning Jaguar in the Jaguar-Daimler Heritage centre, where she was being displayed in 2019. (Author's collection)

This is the view that the TWR Jaguar drivers saw all too often in 1988 ... the rear of the Sauber-Mercedes C9. (Courtesy LAT)

"I think we V-maxed at about 240mph," recalled Martin Brundle. "It's all fine until it's not! Very lazy gearing, long-legged. The Le Mans-bodied cars gather speed really quickly, because they are so slippery through the air.

"Down the Mulsanne you had the tramlines, [depressions] in the road, from the trucks, and when you had to cross the crown of the road for the kink, you'd take it flat but really had to think about it, especially in the middle of the night."

After a month in which to recover and then re-prepare the cars, the field went to Brno in Czechoslovakia. A tremendous 78,000-strong crowd turned out for this chance to see capitalist race teams in their country, and they were not disappointed, even though only 18 cars entered the race.

Two Sauber-Mercedes C9s and two TWR Jaguar XJR-9s were entered for this 360km sprint race, and

Jean-Louis Schlesser claimed his fifth pole position of the year with a 1:46.44. The other team car lined up alongside with a 1:46.70. One Jaguar was third on the grid; the other fifth, with Bob Wollek doing a great job driving the Joest-entered 962.129 and taking fourth on the grid.

When the lights went out, the two Saubers – driven by Mauro Baldi and James Weaver, and Schlesser and Jochen Mass – led, and started to pull away from the Jaguars. But on lap ten, fate took a hand as Baldi suffered a puncture and had to pit. The XJR-9s had not only to contend with the Saubers in this race, but the two Joest Porsche 962Cs also gave them a hard time. Whilst these four were scrapping amongst themselves, the leading Sauber consolidated its lead and, at the end, Mass and Schlesser duly ran out the winners, with Brundle and Nielsen second and Lammers/Dumfries third. The Championship was opening up ...

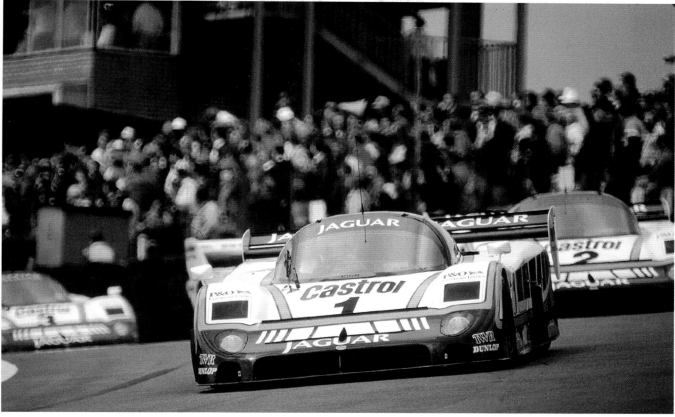

Sweeping into Paddock bend at Brands Hatch in 1988 is the eventual winner, race #1 (XJR-9 588), driven by Martin Brundle, John Nielsen and Andy Wallace, whilst behind them is car #2. Just entering the photo on the left is car #3 (XJR-9, 187), driven by John Watson and Davy Jones. They were also a DNF this time down to the ignition timing failing. (Courtesy John S Allen)

It was back to Britain for the next 1000km race, held at Brands Hatch on July 24th.

Here, during practice, TWR Jaguar had fielded an XJR-9 fitted with twin overhead camshafts per bank and four valves per cylinder. This unit gave a claimed 800bhp, but the extra weight on top of an already tall engine affected the handling adversely and so this engine was not used in the race.

Martin Brundle, interviewed in *Motorsport* said: "The V12 is a very big engine. You definitely do feel the weight. The engines centre of gravity is very important. I remember we tried a 48-valve head with this engine, at Brands Hatch, and although it had a load more power, the car went slower because it altered the centre of gravity."

Despite being only fourth on the grid (Jan Lammers/

Johnny Dumfries), sixth (John Nielsen/Martin Brundle/ Andy Wallace), and eighth (the 48 valve XJR-9 of John Watson and Davy Jones), the Jaguar team knew that the fuel consumption of the turbocharged Saubers and Porsches would bring them into play, but fate dealt them an even better hand when Steve Hynes, driving the 'Pink Panther' Tiga, lost control when being lapped by the Saubers and punted Jochen Mass into retirement, and Mauro Baldi into a spin of his own. It was later on reported that several smirking journalists had witnessed an extremely irate Jochen Mass berating Steve Hynes outside his team's motor home, whilst the Roy Baker mechanics laboured mightily, and succeeded in making the 'Pink Panther' race-worthy again.

It all looked like plain sailing now that the Saubers were effectively out and the Joest Porsche 962C had

At least practice was held in the dry! (Courtesy John S Allen)

slacked off due to its fuel running out, but as the two TWR jaguars were heading for the win, poor Jan Lammers suffered a dashboard fire and had to retire from the lead. This left the XJR-9 of John Nielsen, Andy Wallace and Martin Brundle to take the win, but it had been a very close run race and TWR Jaguar had had to admit that luck had been on its side.

So to the Nürburgring at the beginning of September, where for some unexplained reason, the ADAC organisers chose to run the 1000km race in two heats of 500km each, heat one starting in the evening and finishing in the dark.

Once again, the two Saubers were on the front row, this time with Mauro Baldi as pole sitter, alongside Jean-Louis Schlesser. Bob Wollek in Joest's 962C was third, the two Jaguar XJR-9s finishing up fourth and fifth on the grid.

Come race Saturday and the weather was foul, pouring rain soaking the track and the clerk of the course brought the start time forward by an hour, to allow more racing in the twilight, as against the dark.

The race started under yellow flags to allow drivers to acclimatise themselves to the gloom but when the lights turned green, it was the Sauber that stayed in the lead, with Jean-Louis Schlesser and Jochen Mass leading from the start and heading home Eddie Cheever and Martin

Yes, it really was this bad. Even driving along the straight at the Nürburgring took some doing in 1988. Notice how the drivers have spread out to increase their visibility. Definitely not for the faint-hearted ... (Courtesy John S Allen)

Brundle in their XJR-9. The rain obviously slowed the cars down and the Jaguars undoubtedly lost their fuel mileage advantage. Mauro Baldi and Stefan Johansson had a defective windscreen wiper, and were unable to finish any higher than seventh.

The next day saw the second heat, and the same rain and gloom persisted over the Eifel Mountains. First and second were the same as in the first heat, Dumfries spinning and damaging his rear wing and Baldi doing much the same, putting both cars out of contention.

Spa-Francorchamps on September 18th saw much the same weather as at the Nürburgring: pouring rain. But TWR Jaguar had only to place second to win the Constructors' Championship again, and this it duly did, Jan Lammers and Martin Brundle performing flawlessly.

Brundle's XJR-9 had retired on the 49th lap with fuel pick up problems and so Martin Brundle, who was in line to pick up the Drivers' Championship, duly replaced Johnny Dumfries in the car that he and Jan Lammers usually drove. Jean-Louis Schlesser and Jochen Mass shared the third-placed Sauber, which had suffered from a broken rear wishbone, and the sister car of Mauro Baldi and Stefan Johansson won.

October 9th at Mount Fuji in Japan saw Martin Brundle and Eddie Cheever take a well earned victory, this giving Brundle a richly deserved Drivers' Championship.

Qualifying brought up some startling results, the FromA Porsche 962 of Hideki Okada taking pole, with a March-Nissan R88C taking second place. The Sauber of Mauro Baldi was third, with Toyota fourth. The best that a TWR Jaguar could do was sixth with the sister car seventh. The second Sauber was eighth.

Once the race proper started, the European cars showed their superiority with Brundle leading from the start, but then on lap 35, Jan Lammers had a tyre deflate and visited the barriers, ending his run. Then Jean-Louis Schlesser in the second placed Sauber C9 lost boost pressure and had to pit, where a faulty sensor was diagnosed and replaced. He lost four laps and, unless the British car failed, his chances of winning the drivers' title had gone. The second Sauber then suffered a brake disc failure and was forced into retirement. The race ended with the sole finishing TWR Jaguar the winner, and the best the surviving Sauber C9 could do was fifth.

Martin Brundle duly won the Drivers' Championship, and TWR Jaguar had already won the World Sports Car Championship again.

At West Palm Beach, Jan Lammers and Davy Jones drove this XJR-9, 388 into second place behind Geoff Brabham's Electramotive Nissan GTP car. (Courtesy Lee Self)

So to the final championship race of the year in Australia on November 20th. Sandown, near Melbourne, had seven second-gear corners and was expected to play to the Saubers' strengths. This duly happened, Jean-Louis Schlesser and Jochen Mass pretty much winning as they pleased and Mauro Baldi and Stefan Johansson finishing second. The best that TWR Jaguar could do was third and fourth, with Martin Brundle and Eddie Cheever in the leading car and Jan Lammers and Johnny Dumfries behind.

Also at West Palm in April 1988 was 288, driven by John Nielsen and Martin Brundle. They experienced fuel pressure problems early on, and later the gearbox seized, putting them out of the race. (Courtesy Lee Self)

1988 was another successful year for TWR Jaguar, but the Sauber team, now backed by Mercedes, had looked increasingly threatening as the season wore on. Unless the technicians in Kidlington could unlock more performance from the XJR-9, 1989 was looking a daunting challenge.

Back in America, in the IMSA series, TWR Jaguar may have thought that the win at Daytona was a good indication of how the season would play out, but they had not bargained for the brain power of the Electramotive team, as well as Geoff Brabham's driving skill, aboard the Nissan factory backed Electramotive GTP-ZXT.

Using such tweaks as an electronically controlled wastegate on their turbocharged V6 engine, the Nissan, with Geoff Brabham, usually partnered by John Morton driving, won eight races straight, nine in total, (Road Atlanta, West Palm Beach, Mid-Ohio, Lime Rock,

Watkins Glen, Road America, Portland, and Sears Point), and became the IMSA Champion in 1988. It was not until the last race, held at Del Mar, that TWR Jaguar won again. However, that at least paid $145,000 to the winners.

Davy Jones: "I had been very lucky to race in Formula 3 in Europe in 1983 and 1984 with McLaren. Those were the days of Ayrton Senna and Martin Brundle in F3 and then McLaren, through their involvement with the BMW GTP engine building program in America, helped me get a job driving the Turbocharged BMW GTP cars in 1986. In 1987 I went Indycar racing, and then for 1988 Tony Dowe and Ian Reed, for TWR, asked me to drive the Jaguar-powered GTP cars.

"I first tested for them on the Talladega road course, and Eddie Cheever, Derek Warwick and Jan Lammers were all there. The first time I drove an XJR-9, I found the V12-engined car very heavy, and tried to adapt to it.

Pitstop time for the #60 XJR-9 at Mid-Ohio in June. 288 finished second to Geoff Brabham's Nissan GTP-ZXT again. It was driven by Martin Brundle and John Nielsen. John Nielsen, still in his helmet, can be seen top left. (Courtesy Lee Self)

This car, chassis number 388, finished in third place, driven by Jan Lammers and Davy Jones at Mid-Ohio. (Courtesy Lee Self)

When I came in after my first drive, Roger Silman, the team manager in Europe said to me: 'Davy, just put your foot in it, don't baby it.' Those cars were so stiffly sprung, to counter the ground effect, that you had to drive 'over the edge' to get the best out of them. At the end of that test, I had gone the fastest.

"Incidentally, those V12 engines were bullet proof. They might, over a long race, break a valve spring but they never faltered in their power output. I really enjoyed the XJR-9 and the XJR-12.

"TWR were surprised at how quick the Nissan GTP car was in 1988, but don't forget, they also had an advantage with using Goodyear tyres, which suited the high downforce GTP cars. We were on Dunlops then and we struggled with them, the sidewalls were so stiff and the car bounced a lot."

So for 1988, TWR Jaguar had to settle for third place in the IMSA Camel GTP manufacturers, behind the winning Porsche (by one point, proving the old adage of 'strength in numbers') and Nissan. There was consolation in the fact that John Nielsen finished second in the Drivers' Championship and that between them, he and Martin Brundle earned TWR Jaguar over $300,000 in prize money.

It's possible that TWR had been surprised by the intensity of the racing in IMSA. With none of the fuel consumption rules that bedeviled Group C racing in Europe, the IMSA cars were driven hard all through each race, with no need to back off to preserve fuel consumption. This was a new style of racing, to which the team in America would get used to over the next few years.

XJR-9 – Group C

1988-89 Same basic monocoque, with further detail changes and improved 7.0-litre engine, still using at least one renumbered XJR-6 (186). 6 wins during 1988, including Le Mans. No wins in 1989. 1988 World Teams' and Drivers' Champion (Martin Brundle). Weight 850kg.

XJR-9 – IMSA GTP

1988-89 Same basic car as the Group C version, but with modifications to meet IMSA requirements including a 6.0-litre engine. 2 wins during 1988, the first at the Daytona 24 hours debut on January 30th/31st with Brundle, Nielsen, Lammers and Boesel driving. The next victory was at the last round at Del Mar, California. 1 win in 1989 at Tampa on October 1st (Cobb). The main sponsor was Castrol. Weight 930kg – ballasted to meet IMSA's engine capacity/ configuration rules (later 953kg).

TWR Jaguar XJR-9 (Group C & IMSA GTP 1988)

Constructor Tom Walkinshaw Racing, 1 Station Field, Industrial Estate, Kidlington, Oxford, England

Chassis fabricator Advanced Composite Technology Ltd, Composites House, Adams Close, Heanor Gate Industrial Estate, Heanor, Derbyshire, DE7 7SW

Chassis Carbon fibre and Kevlar monocoque with steel tube supports for engine, designed by Tony Southgate. Single front located Serck water radiator. Twin side mounted Serck oil radiators. Premier fuels Systems Ltd, 100-litre (Group C) 120-litre (IMSA) fuel tank in mid position. 12-litre oil tank in front left-hand side of engine bay.

Body Kevlar, carbon fibre and GRP. Wing and full ground effect underbody in carbon fibre. Underside with regulation flat surfaces and air-ducts as permitted by the regulations (bigger reference surface and lower venturi demanded for Group C cars). Aerodynamics include enclosed rear wheels, except on Le Mans cars, which also have less ground effect and body/wing modification demanded by that circuit.

Engine (Group C) TWR Jaguar 60 degree V12 (Allan Scott) Unblown, liquid cooled 94.0 x 84.0mm/ 6995.3cc Aluminium block and heads Stressed chassis member Wet cast iron liners 7 plain main bearings Nitrided EN40B steel crankshaft with Holset harmonic damper Steel con rods Cosworth alloy pistons. Goetze rings SOHC – single duplex chain driven 2 titanium valves/cylinder, 1 plug (Champion) Zytek engine management and telemetry Bosch injection, Lucas ignition AP 7.25in 3-plate clutch Compression ratio 12.0:1 745bhp at 7250rpm, with peak torque at 615bhp/5500rpm, maximum rpm 7600 Weight 240kg including clutch

Engine (IMSA GTP)
As TWR Group C
V12 except: 94.0 x 72.0mm/ 5996.0cc Titanium con rods. Compression ratio 13.5:1 670bhp at 7500rpm, maximum rpm 7800. 536lb-ft of torque at 6250rpm.

Suspension (front) Wide-base fabricated wishbones actuating pushrods to coil/damper units mounted horizontally at centre-line of the car. Magnesium alloy hub carriers.

Suspension (rear) Magnesium alloy uprights and steel coils. Shock absorbers and brake discs housed

within wheel hubs to allow maximum
venturi width.

AP 4-pot calipers and 13in cast iron brake discs. Dymag 17in
rim Dunlop Denloc kevlar tyres. Koni shocks front, Bilstein
rear.

Gearbox	March/TWR 5 speed, with straight cut gears
General	Cockpit electrically adjustable rear-view mirrors 4 Oscar/Cibie headlamps MRTC radio Lifeline fire system Pipercross air filters Goodridge flexible piping and unions
Dimensions	Wheelbase – 2710mm Length – 4820mm Width – 2020mm Height – 1031mm Front track – 1500mm Rear track – 1450mm
Weight	900kg (Group C) 930kg (IMSA) – 953kg after rule change
Top speed	236mph (Group C Le Mans low-drag trim)

186

1988:
11-12/06: Le Mans 24 hours: D Daly/L Perkins/K Coogan, #22; 4th

With Jaguar Holland, restored

187

1988:
Uprated to XJR-9 spec
06/03: Jerez 800km: J Nielsen/J Watson/A Wallace, #3; 2nd
13/03: Jarama Supersprint: J Nielsen/J Watson, #3; 3rd
24/04: Monza Supersprint: #1T; T car used in practice
08/05: Silverstone 1000km: J Dumfries/ J Lammers, #6; T car replacing 488, DNF (fuel)

10/07: Brno: T car only
24/07: Brands Hatch: J Watson/D Jones, #3; DNF (engine)
Raced with 4 valve engine
Restored and sold to a European collector in 1989
Sold to the Albert Obrist collection in Switzerland
1992: Sold to Bernie Ecclestone
2007: RM Auction

XJR-9 – 188   IMSA car   Castrol colours

1988:
Renumbered from 386
30-31/1: Daytona 24 hrs: E Cheever/J Dumfries/J Watson, #66; 3rd
28/2: Miami GP: R Boesel/E Cheever, #66; DNF (engine)
19/3: Sebring 12 hrs: #60T, T car only
10/4: Road Atlanta: #61T, T car only
24/4: West Palm Beach: #61T, T car only
11-12/6: Le Mans 24 hours: D Sullivan/D Jones/P Cobb, #21; 16th
17/7: Road America: #66, T car only
31/7: Portland: #66, T car only
14/8: Sears Point: #66, T car only
4/9: San Antonio: D Jones/ J Watson, #60; 2nd
2/10: Columbus: D Jones/ J Lammers, #60; 10th
23/10: Del Mar: D Jones/ J Lammers, #61; 1st

See 1989 results

287

1988:
Uprated to XJR-9LM
11-12/06: Le Mans: Watson/Pescarolo/Bell Boesel, #3; DNF (transmission)
04/09: Nürburgring: # 1T; T car only
18/09: Spa-Francochamps: # 1T; T car only

XJR-9 – 288   IMSA car   Castrol colours

1987:
Fall test, Daytona?

1988:
30-31/1: Daytona 24 hours: M Brundle/R Boesel/J Nielsen/ J Lammers, #60; 1st
28/2: Miami GP: M Brundle/J Nielsen, #60; 2nd

19/3: Sebring 12 hours: R Boesel/M Brundle/J Nielsen, #60; DNF (engine)
10/4: Road Atlanta: J Nielsen/J Watson, #60; 2nd
24/4: W Palm Beach: M Brundle/J Nielsen, #60; DNF (transmission)
30/5: Lime Rock: M Brundle/J Nielsen, #60; 2nd
05/6: Mid-Ohio: M Brundle/J Nielsen, #60; 2nd
03/7: Watkins Glen: M Brundle/J Nielsen, #60; DNF (engine)
17/7: Road America: M Brundle/J Nielsen, #60 ; 4th
31/7: Portland: M Brundle/J Nielsen, #60; 3rd
14/8: Sears Point: M Brundle/J Nielsen, #60; 2nd
04/9: San Antonio: J Nielsen/A Wallace, #61; 10th DNF (brakes) classified 10th
2/10: Columbus: M Brundle/J Nielsen, #66; DNF (accident)
23/10: Del Mar: M Brundle/J Nielsen, #66; DNS (accident in practice)
Back to UK for repair

XJR-9 – 388   IMSA car   Castrol colours

1988:
30-31/1: Daytona 24 hours: D Jones/ J Lammers/ D Sullivan, #61;DNF (engine) Classified 26th
28/2: Miami GP: D Jones/J Lammers, #61; 6th
19/3: Sebring 12 hours: J Lammers/D Jones/D Sullivan/J Nielsen #61; 7th
10/4: Road Atlanta:D Jones/A Wallace, #61; 4th
24/4: W Palm Beach: J Lammers/D Jones, #61; 2nd
30/5: Lime Rock: J Lammers/D Jones, #61; 3rd
05/6: Mid-Ohio: J Lammers/D Jones, #61; 3rd
03/7: Watkins Glen: J Lammers/D Jones, #61; DNF (accident), classified 18th
17/7: Road America: J Lammers/D Jones, #61; 5th
31/7: Portland: J Lammers/D Jones, #61; 4th
14/8: Sears Point: J Lammers/D Jones, #61; 3rd
04/9: San Antonio: D Jones/J Watson, #61, Jones crashed heavily in qualifying, did not race
Returned to TWR Kidlington, for repairs

XJR-9 – 488   Group C car   Silk Cut

1988:
06/3: Jerez 800km: J Lammers/ J Dumfries, #2; DNF (G/box)

13/3: Jarama Supersprint: J Lammers/J Dumfries, #2; DNF (spin)
24/4: Monza 1000km; J Lammers/J Dumfries, #2; DNF (Spin)
08/5: Silverstone 1000km: J Lammers/J Dumfries, #2; did not race, car developed faults in practice, 187 used in race
11-12/6: Le Mans 24 hours: J Lammers/J Dumfries/A Wallace, #2; 1st
Retired from racing
In Jaguar Daimler Heritage Collection

XJR-9 – 588   Group C car   Silk Cut

1988:
06/3: Jerez 800km: M Brundle/E Cheever, #1 #2 DNF, (G/Box)
13/3: Jarama Supersprint: M Brundle/E Cheever, #1; 1st
24/4: Monza 1000km: M Brundle/E Cheever, #1; 1st
08/5: Silverstone 1000km: E Cheever/M Brundle, #1; 1st
11-12/6: Le Mans 24 hours: M Brundle/J Nielsen, #1; DNF (Head Gasket)
10/7: Brno: M Brundle/J Nielsen, #1; 2nd
24/7: Brands Hatch: J Nielsen/A Wallace/M Brundle, #1; 1st
3/9: Nürburgring 1000km: E Cheever/M Brundle, #1; 2nd
18/9: Spa-Francorchamps 1000km: E Cheever/ M Brundle, #1; DNF (Fuel system)
Brundle transferred to 688 after 588 retired, to win Teams' Championship
09/10: Fuji 1000km: E Cheever/M Brundle, #1; 1st
20/11: Sandown Park, Australia: M Brundle/E Cheever, #1; 3rd

XJR-9 – 688   Group C car   Silk Cut

1988:
10/7: Brno: J Lammers/J Dumfries, #2; 3rd
24/7: Brands Hatch: J Lammers/J Dumfries, #2; DNF (Electrical)
03/9: Nürburgring 1000km: J Lammers/J Dumfries, #2; 8th
18/9: Spa-Francorchamps 1000km: J Lammers/M Brundle/J Dumfries, #2; 2nd
9/10: Fuji 1000km: J Lammers/J Dumfries, #2; DNF (Acc)
20/11: Sandown Park Australia: J Lammers/J Dumfries, #2; 4th

1989

Looking back now, over 30 years later, at the Group C and GTP racing era, certain things stand out. It can be seen that in 1989, FISA, the endurance racing arm of the FIA, was becoming much more involved than before in what was now a burgeoning series.

Where the politics of motor racing was/is concerned, a little explanation is in order. In Europe, motor racing was and is governed by the FIA, based in Paris, France. In 1904, the national sporting associations (ASN) of nearly all the countries in the world got together and formed an

The number 61 XJR-9D (chassis number 388) was the only one of three TWR entries to see the chequered flag at the 1989 running of the Daytona 24 hours, but, driven by Price Cobb, John Nielsen, Jan Lammers and Andy Wallace, it finished second to a Jim Busby-entered Porsche 962 driven by Derek Bell, Bob Wollek and John Andretti. (Courtesy Lee Self)

XJR-11, chassis number 189, being prepared before a race. A pensive Tom Walkinshaw stands by the cockpit.
(Courtesy John S Allen)

International Automobile Federation (FIA). Among the founder members were the US, France, Great Britain, Germany, and Italy.

This had the beneficial effect of ensuring the same racing classes, circuit and safety standards in all competitions worldwide, for those organisers who wanted to invite competitors from abroad.

Almost uniquely, the US racing clubs had established their own classes and safety standards, such that the original US national sporting authority, the AAA, did not get involved with those standards.

When the AAA decided to leave the FIA, the various clubs who were involved in motorsport such as NASCAR, IMSA, USAC, NHRDA and SCCA formed ACCUS to look after US interests at an international level, but did not generally adopt the FIA world standards for safety, classes, etc, leaving a position where the US uniquely in the world does not to this day accept international standards.

As we have already seen, Group C racing in Europe was effectively a fuel efficiency formula. The cars were allowed a certain amount of fuel to complete a race and, within certain basic parameters, how they did it was down to the teams and manufacturers. What that did was encourage the manufacturers, whose engineers could see the merit of having to make car engines more efficient in fuel burning, leading on to some great advances in street cars, such as electronic fuel-injection, which could meter the amount of fuel used far more efficiently than the old carburettors or mechanically operated fuel-injection.

It can be argued that the FIA effectively killed off

Group C racing in Europe, as by the late 1980s the FIA was under the sway of Bernie Ecclestone, the czar of F1, whose close friend was a certain Max Mosley, the next president of the FIA during this time. Bernie Ecclestone was the boss of the Formula One racing series and it was not in his financial interest to let Group C/Sports car racing prosper, as it took manufacturers and their money, plus spectators away from his series. Hence the plethora of deadening rules which issued from Paris towards the end of the series, such as the institution of the 3.5-litre engine size for 1991, which was not in most car manufacturers' interest.

This was intended to produce what were effectively F1 cars with all-enveloping bodywork, and was not what most car manufacturers wanted at all. They wanted to be able to use modified versions of the engines that powered their road cars, such as the Porsche flat-six that powered the 911/930 range, the Jaguar V12 that powered many of Jaguar's cars and the Mercedes 5-litre V8 that powered the Mercedes, née Sauber Group C cars, again a development of a street car engine.

A specially developed racing 3.5-litre engine was just what Bernie Ecclestone wanted for his F1 cars, however. Hence the FIA doing what it was told by Max and Bernie and this, I would contend, helped to kill off endurance racing in Europe.

Then there was the distance that endurance sports car races were held over. Before 1989, the majority of the races were of 1000km, some 620 miles, or six hours duration. This distance was mandated by the FIA (the Max and Bernie show) to be too long, and was cut back to 480km, or 300 miles, ostensibly to suit television packaging in 1989. This is when the series, as a whole, started to die. The average viewer was not particularly interested in watching sport cars circulating a road course on television for three hours, when they could watch either F1 races at one hour and twenty minutes duration, or NASCAR races where cars did over 200mph – constantly. No, the real fan of endurance races was someone who actually went to the circuits and enjoyed a weekend, or even a day watching cars racing on road courses close up.

It should also be pointed out that spectator attendance at a lot of the 1000km races had in some cases been bad. In fact at some races, the pit personnel outnumbered the sparse amount of spectators ...

But take the case of the biggest and most popular classic sports car race in the world, the Le Mans 24 hours. Thankfully, its organisers, the Automobile Club de l'Ouest, or ACO for short, stood up to FISA, particularly over its demands to own the television rights, and the race even ran outside the FISA's jurisdiction in some years. It didn't hurt either the numbers of the paying public who went there to watch, which were always enormous, nor the amount and quality of the cars entered.

Turning to America, we have to thank John Bishop, who founded IMSA, for such a great series as the GTP era of 1981-1993. John saw that American fans would never stand for a formula that rewarded cars for the frugality of their fuel use, which entailed a lot of cars racing with drivers anxiously watching the fuel gauge. No, he saw that fans wanted to watch drivers and cars going head to head, flat out over the whole distance of the race. One could argue that the American race fan of sports/GTP car racing in the 1980s watched a much more authentic form of racing than their European equivalent.

Everything has its day, and by the early 1990s the writing was on the wall for sports car racing in both Europe and America. A worldwide financial meltdown had occurred in 1988, and that led to manufacturers and teams leaving the series on both sides of the Atlantic. As well, race attendances were hit because spectators couldn't afford to go and watch racing any more, hence the collapse of both Group C in Europe and GTP in America. Motor racing survived, but it was a lean few years in the 1990s.

Back at the TWR base at Kidlington, Tom Walkinshaw was working out, with his engineers, the way to go forward in 1989. If 1987 and 1988 had seen TWR Jaguar dominant, 1989 was, by Tom Walkinshaw's standards, an unmitigated disaster. Probably by most other people's standards it would have been an 'okay' year, but not by Mr Walkinshaw's.

TWR management realised that for the new 480km length 'endurance' races (basically a 'sprint' length by most team's reckoning), TWR needed a more powerful, lighter engine than the tried and trusted V12. It had been using this since 1985 in its Group C cars, and in the Group A XJS since long before that.

The V8 four camshaft engine was made available to TWR at the end of 1988. Originally used in the Austin Metro rally car, this was a four valves per cylinder

To accommodate the new V6, Tony Southgate designed a new carbon fibre chassis and used very similar front and rear suspension to the XJR6-8-9 cars. Downforce for the new XJR-11 was calculated as being 5282lb. The new car was introduced at the race held at Brands Hatch on July 23rd.

It should be noted here that Alan Scott, in charge of TWR's engine design and development, had long urged Tom Walkinshaw to incorporate a machine shop in the engine division, which Tom Walkinshaw steadily refused to countenance. Also, Alan Scott was responsible for just how well the Jaguar V12 engine had been developed in Group C to 7 litres, and IMSA, despite its reduction in size to 6 litres sprung upon TWR just four months before their first race in America.

Tom Walkinshaw seems not to have had complete confidence in Alan Scott's plans to further develop the V12 engine, and indeed, had been planning on using a turbocharged straight six Jaguar AJ6 engine, as developed by Heidegger in Liechtenstein. This was a project that ultimately came to nothing, although Tom Walkinshaw allocated substantial funds towards this end.

Overriding all these decisions being made was also the fact that for 1991, just two short years away, the formula was going to be for naturally aspirated 3.5-litre engines, so striking out with a new engine for those two seasons was, on balance and with the benefit of hindsight (which is always 20/20!), probably the wrong path to go down.

Alan Scott had seen just how well the lightly turbocharged Mercedes V8 engine (as used in the Saubers) did, regarding both acceleration from a corner

The turbocharged 3.0-litre V6 engine of an XJR-10. (Courtesy Lee Self)

The engine bay of the XJR-11. The large size of the radiators required to cool the turbocharged V6 engine are noticeable. (Courtesy John S Allen)

3.5-litre engine and in Group C form would use one turbocharger per bank of three cylinders. Amazingly, its bore and stroke were the same as on TWR's 7-litre V12 engine. Its weight was only 143kg, as against the V12 engine's 240kg.

A sea of purple and white. The TWR team at Le Mans in 1989, prior to the race, lining up for the official photo.
(Courtesy John S Allen)

and fuel consumption, with the Bosch Motronic 1.7 system. Also, Scott had developed the V12 Jaguar engine to its present success, and regarded development of that engine as the path for the next two years. However, it appears that Tom Walkinshaw saw a highly turbocharged six-cylinder engine of smaller capacity, as in the Porsche 962, as the way to go. Scott tried in vain to point out to Walkinshaw that this was just the type of engine, as used in Porsche 962s, that TWR had beaten with its big V12s.

There was also the fact that the type of fuel specified by the FIA, up to 98 RON, suited the naturally aspirated Jaguar engine. Previously Porsche had been able to avail itself of exotic highly aromatic fuels to help develop its power, but that avenue had now been blocked.

Before the new XJR-11 was introduced (and used alongside it), TWR used its now very well developed XJR-9, suitably upgraded for 1989. The XJR-11 had been designed to take 18in diameter wheels for Dunlop's

Almost a home race. The British fans have always treated Le Mans as almost 'their' race. Note the hand written poster message to FISA. The British have never liked bureaucracy. (Courtesy John S Allen)

new radial tyres, as against the 19in diameter ones on the XJR-9 for the previous year's crossply tyres. Sadly, Dunlop's new radials were not as good as perhaps they should have been, with the result that the TWR run cars did not have the grip to match the opposition. In desperation, TWR tried to go back to the 1988 set up but couldn't, as the suspension had been redesigned to take the new smaller diameter wheels. The new Group C Nissan, designed and built by Lola, also suffered from Dunlop's lack of readiness for the 1989 season, and a

switch to Goodyear for the following season was needed to put matters back in order for Jaguar.

The first race of the FIA World Sports Prototype Championship of drivers and teams (what a mouthful!) was at Suzuka on April 9th, and here the home country Toyotas took the first row. The second row held Jan Lammer's and Patrick Tambay's Jaguar, whilst fifth on the grid was Mauro Baldi's Sauber, now painted in Mercedes silver, with no sponsorship showing. Mike Thackwell was in the other Sauber, set to drive the whole race single-

Chassis number 688 being unloaded from its covered trailer at the beginning of Le Mans week in June,1989.
(Courtesy John S Allen)

handed as his co-driver, Jochen Mass had been taken ill and did not do the race. Thackwell had to start from 30th on the grid in a car that he had not driven before. It was a measure of his ability that he sliced through the field, and when the leader, Mauro Badi, pitted for tyres, he actually led the race until being told to drop back behind the Jean-Louis Schlesser/Mauro Baldi Sauber to allow them to take the win and maximum points. The best that TWR could salvage was fifth with John Nielsen and Andy Wallace, whilst Jan Lammers and Patrick Tambay's lack of grip resulted in them running out of fuel on the last lap. It was not a good portent ...

It was back to home ground on May 13th for the next race at Silverstone, but as this was now not a race in which championship points could be won, neither TWR Jaguar nor the Sauber-Mercedes teams bothered to attend. It turned into a privateer Porsche 962 benefit, with no less than six of them placing in the top ten, including the winning Joest-entered 962 of Bob Wollek.

Dijon-Prenois on May 21st saw the next championship race, and the usual suspects were all there, including TRW-Jaguar, Mercedes, Nissan, Toyota, Mazda and Aston-Martin. Pole was duly taken by Jean-Louis Schlesser in 1:07:27, with Johnny Dumfries second in a TOMS Toyota 88C, just 0.4 seconds slower. Due to their tyre troubles, the best that the two XJR-9s could do was seventh and ninth. Sauber-Mercedes' Michelins were also troublesome, the two C9s placing second and third, some 38 seconds behind the winning Joest Porsche 962, which was on Goodyear tyres. Bob Wollekand and Frank Jelinski were driving the same car that had won at Silverstone the week before.

One of the two finishers for TWR Jaguar at Le Mans in 1989 was 287, an XJR-9LM. It is seen here in the paddock shortly after being delivered. (Courtesy John S Allen)

The two TWR Jaguar XJR-9s had a torrid time, Lammers running out of fuel yet again on the last lap whilst placed fourth, and Andy Wallace crashing the sister car when a tyre deflated.

This year, Le Mans was held on June 10th-11th, and, despite being outside the championship, it had its usual completely full entry list. One wonders at the idiocy of the FIA organisers in Paris not being able to come to terms with the organisers of Le Mans, the Automobile Club de l'Ouest. It was up to both organisations – the FIA more than the ACO – to come to an amicable agreement over the television rights.

TWR Jaguar brought four cars for the race, whilst Sauber Mercedes brought three, one of which, driven by Jean-Louis Schlesser, took pole position at 3:15:04. At least TWR Jaguar made the second row: Jan Lammers, Patrick Tambay and Andrew Gilbert-Scott, and the other XJR-9 driven by Davy Jones, Derek Daly and Jeff Kline.

At the finish, the Sauber-Mercedes C9 of Jochen Mass, Manual Reuter and Stanley Dickens won. In second place was the second team car of Mauro Baldi, Kenny Acheson and Gianfranco Brancatelli, with Jean-Louis Schlesser, Alain Cudini and Jean-Pierre Jabouille fifth.

The TWR team spent the race fixing problems that occurred on its cars, mainly gearbox-related. The 'best of the rest' was the XJR-9 of Jan Lammers, Patrick Tambay and Andrew Gilbert-Scott. At one point during the night Lammers had led the race with this car, chassis number 588, but was delayed by the aforementioned gearbox problems and two broken exhausts. At least the 'French' car of Alain and Michel Ferté, and Eliseo Salazar had

The turbocharged V6-engined XJR-11
at Brands Hatch in 1989. It was fast
in practice, but suffered in the race.
More development was needed.
(Courtesy John S Allen)

▼ ▲ *Race number 2 at Le Mans, 688, was driven by John Nielsen, Andy Wallace and Price Cobb. It retired when a head gasket failed after 215 laps.*
(Courtesy John S Allen)

finished eighth and Alain Ferté had posted fastest lap of the race in a 3:21:27.

Regarding the gearbox problems, it later transpired that they had mistakenly been filled with engine oil ... The 1989 race was also a tragedy for the TWR team, as Steve Harding, one of their engine builders, was killed whilst crossing a road in France.

The rest of the season is simply told. At Jarama for the next round the Sauber-Mercedes C9 of Schlesser and Mass won, but at least the second car across the line was the XJR-9 of Jan Lammers and Patrick Tambat, despite being lapped on their uncompetitive tyres.

Brands Hatch on July 23rd saw the debut of the V6 turbocharged engine XJR-11. Things looked good to begin with, as Jan Lammers took pole with 1:12:927, putting the two Sauber-Mercedes C9s into second and third places on the grid. The second XJR-11 started fifth with Davy Jones, but the old XJR-9, although with bad tyres, started 11th. Even the older Porsche 962s were faster ...

PROGRAMME OFFICIEL

24 HEURES DU MANS

10-11 JUIN 1989

35 F

AUTOMOBILE CLUB DE L'OUEST

LES FORCES

60 voitures représentant 15 constructeurs et 31 équipes sont engagées pour ces 57es « 24 Heures ». Le gage d'une course animée même si la sortie de l'épreuve du Championnat du Monde des voitures sport prototype a troublé jusqu'au dernier moment le bel ordonnancement de la liste des présents. Une fois encore Porsche avec 18 voitures, est le mieux représenté, devant Spice dont 10 machines sont attendues. Forte présence des usines Jaguar, Mercedes, Nissan, Toyota et Mazda qui seront représentées par au moins trois voitures alors que le constructeur local Yves Courage et Aston Martin compteront sur deux C1 chacun pour faire entendre leurs voix.

Team Silk Cut Jaguar

Les grands vainqueurs de la saison 88, qui, outre les deux titres mondiaux Pilotes et Equipes, avaient réussi le double Daytona-Le Mans. Une domination totale la monopole durant la première demi-saison avant que les Sauber-Mercedes ne « mettent le turbo ». Après une fin de saison relativement équilibrée entre les deux parties, avantage très net en 89 au camp suisse-

allemand et surtout déroute des Britanniques qui n'ont même pas pu conduire une XJR 9 à l'arrivée il y a deux semaines à Dijon. Malgré cela, Tom Walkinshaw reste confiant pour les 24 Heures. « Nous avons établi un record de distance, un record de vitesse moyenne et il n'y a pas de raison que nous ne renouvelions pas ces performances. » Jaguar est donc candidat à sa propre succession, ce qui ne surprendra pas grand-monde si l'on se penche sur le palmarès de la classique française. Hormis Lagonda (1935), Delahaye (1938), Talbot (1950), Mercedes (1952), Aston Martin (1959), Mirage (1975), Renault (1978) et Rondeau (1980), les 48 autres victoires sont à partager entre dix constructeurs seulement ! Dans la Sarthe, le succès sont à répétition. Pour justifier cette prévision, Walkinshaw a engagé quatre modèles quasiment identiques à la XJR 9 gagnante il y a douze mois. Par rapport à une version « sprint », cela se traduit par un aileron arrière positionné beaucoup plus bas, des tunnels déporteurs exploités au maximum, un moteur acceptant les reprises à bas régime et une boîte aux rapports particulièrement étudiés de façon à consommer le moins possible. Cette année, les Jaguar bénéficient par ailleurs de pneus Dunlop de 18" (et non plus 17" comme par le passé) et de freins dont le diamètre a été porté à 14". Titulaire de quatre engagements, la firme de Coventry a, comme en 1988, résolu un problème de pilotes. Quatre titulaires en championnat du monde (Tambay, Lammers, Wallace et Nielsen) plus les deux représentants Jaguar en I.M.S.A. (Cobb et Jones), restait à trouver la moitié de l'effectif. Pour des raisons de disponibilité autant que promotionnelles, le complément sera très international avec les « Français » de Falaise (Alain et Michel Ferté), le Chilien Eliseo Salazar, l'Américain Jeff Kline, l'Irlandais Derek Daly et le Britannique (tout de même) A. Gilbert-Scott. Toujours sponsorisées par les cigarettes Silk Cut, Castrol et Dunlop, les Jaguar recevront le soutien inconditionnel de 30 000 à 40 000 supporters venus de Grande-Bretagne en particulier mais aussi de toute l'Europe, voire des Etats-Unis.

31

The cover of the programme for the Le Mans 24 hours in 1989. (Courtesy John Gabrial)

Coverage of the TWR Jaguars at Le Mans in the programme for 1989. (Courtesy John Gabrial)

Race number 1 at Brands Hatch in 1989 was the XJR-11 driven by Jan Lammers and Patrick Tambay. They finished fifth. (Courtesy John S Allen)

Despite losing out at the start, and suffering damage to an exhaust pipe, which damaged the turbocharger on that side, Jan Lammers and Patrick Tambay finished fifth, behind the two Saubers, one of which won, the Porsche 962C of Bob Wollek and Frank Jelinski and, surprisingly, the Aston-Martin AMR-1 in fourth place of David Leslie and Brian Redman, which simply rumbled around without having any problems.

A fuel problem forced XJR-11 (chassis number 289, race number 2, driven by Andy Wallace and Alain Ferté) out of the race at Donington in August. (Courtesy John S Allen)

The new XJR-11, seen here at Brands Hatch. (Courtesy John S Allen)

The TWR garage in the pits at Donington in 1989. (Courtesy John S Allen)

Amazingly, after the previous year's torrential rain, the Nürburgring was sunny and warm for the whole weekend of August 20th, when the circus turned up for the next race. Here the two Sauber-Mercedes C9s did their usual, dominating the front row positions, whilst Jan Lammers lined up third. There were two XJR-11s entered here, no V12s in sight for the first time in four years. The XJR-11 of John Nielsen and Andy Wallace had an oil fire in practice that virtually destroyed the rear end, giving the mechanics an all-nighter to ready the car for the race.

At the end of the race, it was this car that finished best, taking a well earned fifth slot, being beaten by the two Saubers taking the first two places, followed by the Kremer-entered Porsche 962C of Fouche and Lavaggi, and the Walter Brun entered 962C of Brun himself, with Jesus Pareja coming fourth. Jan Lammers and Patrick Tambay finished in tenth place. Andy Wallace remembered: "Where the V12 cars were concerned, there was no boost control to turn up, so we always lost out to the Saubers and the Porsches in qualifying. But those turbo cars ... the power was all at the top end, not like the V12s, which

Jan Lammers and Patrick Tambay drove XJR-11, chassis number 189 at Donington in 1989. They retired after 45 laps with electrical problems. (Courtesy John S Allen)

had a much more even power spread. You really needed to be on top of the XJR-10 and 11 to get them to work. They were pretty vicious-difficult!"

Sauber-Mercedes was now in a completely dominant position, whilst TWR Jaguar was trying to come to grips with a new design, bad tyres and high fuel consumption.

Mercedes had dominated proceedings at Donington on 3rd September 1939, and exactly 50 years later to the day, it did it again, taking first and second and the Teams' Championship. Lammers put up a strong fight, but the distributor drive broke on the 39th lap, and he and Patrick Tambay were out.

A Sauber-Mercedes C9 won again at Spa-Francorchamps on September 17th, but it was not the car of Jean-Louis Schlesser – it was that of team-mate Mauro Baldo, with Kenny Acheson as his co-driver. Schlesser had been leading but ran out of fuel on the last lap. Once again, Jan Lammers had driven a spirited race in his XJR-11, taking third on the grid, ahead of John Nielsen in the other car in third place. They were soon out of the race, Lammers on lap 16 with a blown turbocharger and Nielsen with a flat battery on lap 26. Nevertheless, they had displayed excellent handling.

Jean-Louis Schlesser became World Sports Prototype Champion on October 29th at Mexico City, when he won the race outright. Mauro Baldi, his team-mate, would have had to win the race to win the Championship but that didn't happen as Kenny Acheson, Baldi's co-driver, in trying catch Schlesser, crashed the Sauber on lap 46. TWR had sent two XJR-9s, for some reason not bothering with the XJR-11s in this, the last race of 1989. At least they managed to finish fifth and sixth, Andy Wallace and Alain Ferté just beating out Jan Lammers and Patrick Tambay, both finishing on the same lap, one lap down on the winner.

And so we move over to America, for the IMSA season of 1989. There, TWR Jaguar placed second no less than seven times but at least they won three races, two of them at Portland and Del Mar with their new, 3.0-litre turbocharged V6 engine in the new XJR-10. Jan Lammers was the common denominator in both races, his co-driver at Portland was Price Cobb, who drove the winning XKR-9 at the Florida State Fairgrounds race and at Del Mar, Jan Lammers drove solo. TWR Jaguar also managed to take seven second places, placing them second in the Manufacturers' Championship, with Price Cobb placing third in the Drivers' Championship, behind

Some People Wonder Why Jaguar Races. We Wonder Why Others Don't.

The IMSA Camel GTP Championship is one of the most challenging series in auto racing. It tests a car company's ability and spirit to the very core.

That's exactly why Jaguar races in the IMSA series. We find the IMSA Camel GTP series to be the perfect testing ground for many Jaguar improvements. After all, traveling at 200 mph reveals an awful lot about the way a car works.

And while victories at the 24 Hours of Daytona and LeMans, as well as consecutive World Sports Car Championships in 1987 and 1988 are certainly satisfying, it's what racing teaches us that is most important.

You'll find this knowledge and racing spirit echoed in all of our 1990 Jaguars, from the luxurious XJ6, Sovereign and Vanden Plas sedans, to our V12-powered XJ-S coupes and convertibles.

Test drive a Jaguar. For your nearest dealer call 1-800-4-JAGUAR. And remember, every time the Castrol Jaguar races, you win.

JAGUAR

A BLENDING OF ART AND MACHINE

Jaguar wasted no time in using the new XJR-10s debut to its advantage when it came to advertising ...
(Courtesy 1989 IMSA Yearbook)

Geoff Brabham and Chip Robinson, who drove the second Nissan.

Otherwise, up till Lime Rock on May 29th, when the XJR-10 was introduced, the 'old' 6.0-litre XJR-9 had been the team's weapon. Once again, as in 1988, the Electramotive Nissan GTP ZXT steamrollered the opposition, again with the principal driver being Geoff Brabham. They won ten races out of fourteen and the Drivers' and Constructors' Championship.

The opening 24-hour race at Daytona saw a thrilling finish; the Nissan had led for most of the first 18 hours but then retired with mechanical problems. From then till the finish the Castrol-sponsored XJR-9 of Andy Wallace, Price Cobb, John Nielsen and Jan Lammers engaged in a battle with the Miller High Life-sponsored BFG Porsche 962, driven by Bob Wollek, John Andretti, and Derek Bell finally beating the XJR-9 by just 86 seconds. That 962 itself was highly modified from that which had left the Porsche factory in 1985, being built upon an 'aftermarket' chassis and having numerous modifications to make it competitive.

Nissan did not have as easy a year in 1989 as it had had in 1988. At Miami, for instance, Geoff Brabham and co-driver Chip Robinson only beat the XJR-9 of Price Cobb and John Nielsen by seven seconds.

The Sebring 12 hours was dominated by Geoff Brabham and Chip Robinson, but again, Price Cobb and John Nielsen were second in their XJR-9. It was the same story at the following race at Road Atlanta. Electramotive Nissan first, TWR Jaguar second.

Palm Beach saw a change in the Nissan's winning streak when it's engine blew after just four laps. A scrap then ensued between the TWR Jaguar XJR-9 of Price Cobb and John Nielsen, and the Miller High Life BFG Porsche 962 and driving it, Bob Wollek and John Andretti took their second win of the season, with the Jaguar again in second place. Another threat, both to TWR Jaguar and Electramotive was the Eagle Toyota of Dan Gurney's team, which led for part of this race, as did the Pontiac Firebird (Spice) of Costas Los and Jean-Louis Ricci. At this point in the IMSA Championship, TWR Jaguar was leading on points ...

Jan Lammers introduced the TWR Jaguar XJR-10 at Lime Rock and gave it a good debut, but he was still beaten into second place by the Nissan of Geoff Brabham, with the XJR-9 of Price Cobb and John Nielsen taking third place.

It was the same result at Mid-Ohio, only this time it was John Nielsen and Price Cobb driving the XJR-9, eight seconds behind. Jan Lammers' XJR-10 had retired at two thirds distance with "cooling problems."

Davy Jones and Jan Lammers drove the XJR-9 and XJR-10 respectively at Watkins Glen, the next race, but Jones retired after just four laps and Lammers after 32, both with engine trouble. The Nissan won again ...

The fast Road America circuit in Wisconsin saw yet another Nissan victory, and the two Jaguars – Jan Lammers and Price Cobb in the XJR-10, and John Nielsen and Davy Jones – finished second and third respectively, all three cars being on the lead lap at the finish.

And then came Portland, where Jan Lammers won and John Nielsen was fourth in the XJR-9, sandwiching the two Nissans in second and third. This time, all four of these cars were on the lead lap at the end of the race. That's what the results said, but what actually happened was that the chequered flag was thrown three laps before the end, when the Jaguar was leading. Geoff Brabham then overtook Jan Lammers and took the flag three laps later, at the correct distance. One can imagine the protests. It's probable that Lammers slacked off on seeing the flag and that allowed the Nissan to overtake him. The result went to a court case, but TWR Jaguar got the nod.

Topeka came next on the 13th August, and it was back to the status quo, Geoff Brabham taking the victory, Chip Robinson in the sister car placing second and Jan Lammers' XJR-10 taking third. At San Antonio at the beginning of September, Chip Robinson in the one Nissan won, whilst Geoff Brabham in the other car, Michel Ferté in the TWR XJR-9 and Davy Jones in the XJR-10 were all non-finishers, Jones with engine problems, Ferté after an accident, and Brabham with a blown engine.

The season was winding down now but there was still all to play for and the Nissans were back on top again at Sears Point on 10th of September, where the two Nissans of Geoff Brabham and Chip Robinson finished first and second and the XJR-9 of Davy Jones and John Nielsen were third, Price Cobb and Jan Lammers taking fourth place. Florida State Fairgrounds in Tampa at the beginning of October saw Price Cobb win in the XJR-9 whilst, uncharacteristically, both Nissans hit trouble and could only finish in fourth and sixth places. Geoff Brabham had had a long pit stop, putting Chip Robinson

into the lead but, seven laps from the end, under pressure, Robinson spun and Cobb won. Jan Lammers in the XJR-10 finished tenth after being involved in an accident.

Finally, the last race of 1989 saw Jan Lammers taking victory at Del Mar in California, together with a record purse of $182,500, with Geoff Brabham in second place and another XJR-10, that of Price Cobb, taking seventh.

It was not a bad season, but the XJR-10 didn't seem to be quite as fast as the Nissan, Geoff Brabham managing to pull out the stops where and when it counted to take another deserved championship.

◀ ▼ ▶　*Three views of Jaguar XJR-9, in July, 1989 at Road America. Once again, it was Price Cobb and Jan Lammers beaten into second place by the Electramotive Nissan GTP car. The other XJR-9, driven by John Nielsen and Davy Jones, was third. (Courtesy Lee Self)*

I raced the street XJR-15 at Monaco, where I came second to
Derek Warwick, and at Silverstone. I missed Spa because of a
clash in commitments. I liked that car.

DAVY JONES

XJR-9 – 188

1989:
4-5/2: Daytona 24 hours: D Daly/M Donnelly/P Tambay, #66; DNF. (Accident, classified 67th)
5/3: Miami GP: #66, T car only
18/3: Sebring 12hrs: #66, T car only
2/4: Road Atlanta: D Jones, #66, badly damaged a week before the race and sent to UK for repairs

1990:
Sold to Mr Manfred Lipman, USA
In Imperial Palace Collection, Las Vegas
Renumbered to 991

XJR-9 – 287

1989:
10-11/06: Le Mans 24 hours: A Ferté/E Salazar/M Ferté, #4; 8th.
23/07: Brands Hatch: # 1T; T car only
29/10: Mexico City: A Wallace/A Ferté, #2; 5th
In TWR Collection

2004:
Sold to European collector

2005:
Raced in Group C – GTP in Europe

XJR-9 – 288

1989:
4-5/2: Daytona 24 hours: J Lammers/R Boesel/D Jones, #60; DNF (engine)
05/3: Miami GP: D Jones/J Lammers, #60; DNF (accident) classified 43rd
18/3: Sebring 12 hours: D Jones/J Lammers, #60; 14th
02/4: Road Atlanta: D Jones/J Lammers, #60; DNF (engine) classified 16th
23/4: W. Palm Beach: D Jones/J Lammers, #60; DNF (transmission)
10-11/6: Le Mans 24 hours: D Jones/J Kline/D Daly, #3; DNF (engine)
Renumbered to 790

1989:
13/8: Topeka: M Ferté, #66T, T car only
03/9: San Antonio: M Ferté/ D Jones, #66T, used practice session only
10/9: Sears Point: D Jones/J Nielsen, #60; 3rd
1/10: Tampa: P Cobb, #60; 1st

XJR-9 – 388
Returned to UK for repairs

1989:
4-5/2: Daytona 24 hours: P Cobb/J Nielsen/A Wallace/J Lammers, #61; 2nd
05/3: Miami GP: P Cobb/J Nielsen, #61; 2nd
18/3: Sebring 12 hours: J Nielsen/P Cobb, #61; 2nd
02/4: Road Atlanta: P Cobb/J Nielsen, #61; 2nd
23/4: W. Palm Beach: P Cobb/J Nielsen, #61; 2nd
29/5: Lime Rock: P Cobb/J Nielsen, #61; 3rd
04/6: Mid-Ohio: P Cobb/J Nielsen/D Jones, #61; 2nd
02/7: Watkins Glen: D Jones/J Nielsen, #61; (engine) classified 18th
16/7: Road America: J Nielsen/D Jones, #61; 3rd
30/7: Portland: J Nielsen/D Jones, #61; 4th
13/8: Topeka: D Jones/J Nielsen, #60; 5th
3/9: San Antonio: M Ferté/J Nielsen, #60; DNF (accident) classified 22nd
Car sent to UK for repairs, upgraded to XJR-12D for 1990

XJR-9 – 588

1989:
9/04: Suzuka: J Lammers/P Tambay, #1; DNF (fuel)
21/5: Dijon: J Lammers/P Tambay, #1; DNF (fuel)
10-11/6: Le Mans 24 hours: J Lammers/P Tambay/A Gilbert-Scott, #1; 4th
25/6: Jarama: J Lammers/P Tambay, #1; 2nd
20/8: Nürburgring: J Nielsen; #1T DNS. T-car
03/9: Donington: 1T: DNS. T-car
17/9: Spa-Francorchamps: A Wallace/J Nielsen, #2T; DNS T-car
29/10: Mexico City: J Lammers/P Tambay, #1; 6th

XJR-9 688

1989:
9/04: Suzuka: J Nielsen/A Wallace, #2; 5th
21/5: Dijon: J Nielsen/A Wallace, #2; DNF (tyres)

10-11/6: Le Mans 24 hours: J Nielsen/A Wallace/P Cobb, #2; DNF (head gasket)
25/6: Jarama: J Nielsen/A Wallace, #2; 6th
23/7: Brands Hatch: J Nielsen/A Wallace, #2; DNF (accident)
Back to TWR for repair
In TWR collection

2003:
Sold to Aaron Hsu

2004:
Sold

XJR10-11

Constructor	Tom Walkinshaw Racing, 1 Station Field Industrial Estate, Kidlington, Oxford, England.
Chassis fabricator	Advanced Composite Technology Ltd., Composites House, Adams Close, Heanor Gate Industrial Estate, Heanor, Derbyshire, DE7 7SW
Chassis	Carbon fibre and kevlar monocoque with steel tube supports for engine, designed by Tony Southgate. Single front located Serck water radiator. Twin side mounted Serck oil radiators. Premier fuels Systems Ltd, 100 litre (Group C) 120-litre (IMSA) fuel tank in mid position. 12-litre oil tank in front left-hand side of engine bay
Body	Kevlar, carbon fibre and GRP. Wing and full ground effect underbody in carbon fibre. Underside with regulation flat surfaces and air-ducts as permitted by the regulations (bigger reference surface and lower venturi demanded for Group C cars)
Engine (Group C)	Rover V64V 90 degree V6 (Allan Scott) Twin Garrett turbochargers, liquid cooled. 94.0 x 84.0mm/ 3498cc. Aluminium block and heads. Stressed chassis member. Wet cast iron liners. 4 valves per cylinder. 1 plug (Champion). Steel con rods. Cosworth alloy pistons. Goetze rings. DOHC – belt driven. Zytek engine management and telemetry. (Bosch from 1990). Bosch Fuel-injection, Lucas ignition.760bhp at 7500rpm, with peak torque at 615 bhp/6000rpm. Maximum rpm 7600. Weight 143kg including clutch
Engine (IMSA GTP)	As TWR Group C V6 except:-94.0 x 72.0mm/ 3000.0cc. Titanium con rods. Compression ratio 13.5:1650bhp at 7500rpm. Maximum rpm 7800
Suspension (front)	Wide-base fabricated wishbones actuating pushrods to coil/damper units mounted horizontally at centre-line of the car. Magnesium alloy hub carriers
Suspension (rear)	Magnesium alloy uprights and steel coils. Shock absorbers and brake discs housed within wheel hubs to allow maximum venturi width
	AP 4-pot calipers and 13in cast iron brake discs. Dymag 18in rims, with Dunlop Denloc kevlar tyres. Koni shocks front, Bilstein rear
Gearbox	March/TWR 5 speed, with straight cut gears
General	Cockpit electrically adjustable rear-view mirrors. 4 Oscar/Cibie headlamps. MRTC radio. Lifeline fire system. Pipercross air filters. Goodridge flexible piping and unions.
Dimensions	Wheelbase – 2710mm Length – 4820mm Width – 2020mm Height – 1031mm Front track – 1500mm Rear track – 1450mm
Weight	900kg (Group C) 930kg (IMSA) – 953kg after rule change
Top speed	236mph (Group C)

XJR-11 – 189   3.5-litre twin-turbo Group C Silk Cut

1989:
23/7: Brands Hatch: J Lammers/P Tambay, #1; 5th
20/8: Nürburgring: J Lammers/P Tambay, #1; 10th
03/9: Donington: J Lammers/P Tambay, #1; DNF (ignition, electrics)
17/9: Spa-Francorchamps: J Lammers/P Tambay, #1; DNF (turbo, engine)
Renumbered to 1390 for 1990

XJR-11 – 289   3.5-litre twin-turbo Group C Silk Cut

1989:
23/7: Brands Hatch: D Jones/A Ferté, #3; DNF (ignition)
20/8: Nürburgring: J Nielsen/A Wallace, #2; 5th
03/9: Donington: A Wallace/A Ferté, #2; DNF (electrics)
Renumbered to 590 for Silverstone race in May, 1990

XJR-10 – 389   3-litre twin turbo IMSA Castrol

1989
29/5: Lime Rock: J Lammers, #60; 2nd
04/6: Mid-Ohio: J Lammers/D Jones, #60; DNF (o/heating)
02/7: Watkins glen: J Lammers/P Cobb, #60; DNF (puncture)
16/7: Road America: J Lammers/ P Cobb, #60; 2nd
30/7: Portland: J Lammers/P Cobb, #60; 1st
13/8: Topeka: P Cobb/J Lammers, #61; 3rd
3/9: San Antonio: P Cobb/J Lammers, #61; DNF (engine) classified 25th
10/9: Sears point: P Cobb/J Lammers, #61; 4th
1/10: Tampa: J Lammers, #61; DNF (accident) classified 9th
22/10: Del mar: J Lammers, #60; 1st

XJR-10 – 489   3-litre twin turbo IMSA Castrol

1989
30/7: Portland: D Jones, #66; DNF (mech)
13/9: Topeka P Cobb/J Lammers, not raced, used in practice only
17/8 Grattan, MI: Testing – destroyed (fire)

XJR-10 – 589   3-litre twin turbo IMSA Castrol

1989:
22/10: Del Mar: P Cobb, #61; 7th

The XJR-15, although not a Group C car, was designed as a road car in 1989/1990, but capable of being raced on the track. It was used in a one-off racing series in Europe.

Using the XJR-9 as a base, Peter Stevens was enlisted by Tom Walkinshaw to make a car to rival Jaguar's XJ220 and Stevens penned a very attractive carbon fibre/Kevlar body to mount upon the XJR-9 carbon fibre chassis. The cockpit was widened by 75mm and the roof heightened by 40mm, to give more space in the cockpit. A V12 engine with a Group C bottom end and Group A heads was used. Originally, the car was called the 'R-9R.' The original design was in clay by October, 1989 but race preparation of the XJRs kept completion back. The first one was completed by July,1989, in time for Tom Walkinshaw to drive it on his return from the race at Le Mans. The original price was £500,000 and Jaguar Sport, in Bloxham, England built 53 of them. The car weighed just 2315lb, about the same as a small hatchback. Top speed was geared to 191mph, and 0 to 60mph was 3.2 seconds.

The XJR-15 was raced in its own series, the Jaguar Intercontinental Challenge, supporting the F1 races at Monaco, Silverstone and Spa. Armin Hahne was the winning driver and took home US$1m in prize money.

Davy Jones: "I raced the street XJR-15 at Monaco, where I came second to Derek Warwick, and at Silverstone. I missed Spa because of a clash in commitments. I liked that car."

Nissan Motorsports rebodied several XJR-15s and called them Nissan R390 GT1s. At the 19998 running of the Le Mans 24 hours race, they placed third, fifth, sixth and tenth places overall, after they had been developed by TWR.

Engine	
Type	Naturally aspirated 60° V12
Construction	Aluminium-alloy block and heads, forged-alloy pistons, nitrided forged EN40B steel crankshaft with Holset harmonic damper, seven main bearings, cast iron 'wet' cylinder liners, Cosworth pistons
Bore X Stroke	90mm × 78.5mm (3.54in × 3.09in)
Valvetrain	Operated by single overhead camshaft per bank of cylinders, two valves per cylinder
Fuel System	Zytek fuel-injection and electronic engine management
Displacement	5993cc (6.0 L; 365.7cu in)

Compression ratio	11.0:1
Max power	450bhp (336kW; 456PS) at 6250rpm
Max. Torque	420lb-ft (569Nm) at 4500rpm
Engine weight	299kg (659lb) including clutch and accessories

Transmission

Type	TWR 5-speed manual (with synchromesh)
Gear Ratio 1st	3.00:1
Gear Ratio 2nd	2.13:1
Gear Ratio 3rd	1.66:1
Gear Ratio 4th	1.38:1
Gear Ratio 5th	1.18:1
Gear Ratio 6th	0.91:1
Final drive ratio	2.90:1
	AP carbon triple-plate clutch

Body

Body/frame type	Carbon fibre
Body/chassis details	Carbon fibre and Kevlar composite construction monocoque chassis with engine used as rear suspension load bearer; lightweight composite and carbon fibre reinforced body with under-surface adopting ground-effect, venturi channels, to the rear and regulation flat floor (race trim)
Coefficient of drag	0.30
Weight distribution	48% front, 52% rear
Wheels/tyres	17in OZ forged alloy wheels (9.5 front/13 rear), Pirelli P Zero tyres

Performance

0-60mph	3.2 seconds
Top speed	307km/h (191mph)
Power to weight ratio	429.39hp/tonne

A note should be made here about the XJ220. This was a supercar conceived and first built by Jaguar engineers in their spare time, led by Jim Randle. It was a V12 engined car when it was first shown to the public at the British Motor Show, held at the NEC in 1988, to rave reviews, and Jaguar took many deposits.

By 22nd February 1989, Tom Walkinshaw had agreed a contract with Jaguar to produce up to 350 cars and 400 engines, starting with 200 cars in the first year of production, 1990. It was seen by TWR staff as yet one more distraction from their main job of producing, developing and racing Group C and IMSA cars.

The subsequent history of the XJ220 is well known; the financial meltdown of the world's economy meant a relatively short production run of 275 cars, and even then problems with the V12 engine led to it being replaced with a turbocharged V6, which resulted in many prospective owners wanting their deposits back – yet another distraction for Tom Walkinshaw.

Three XJ220-Cs, as they were known, did race at the Le Mans 24 hours in 1993, and one of them, driven by David Coulthard, John Nielsen and David Brabham won the GT class, beating old rival, Porsche. Sadly, it was later on disqualified for not running with catalytic converters, with which it had been homologated. Jaguar appealed against this decision and won, but the ACO nevertheless still excluded the result, saying that the appeal had not been lodged in time.

Chapter 7

XJR-10-11 1990

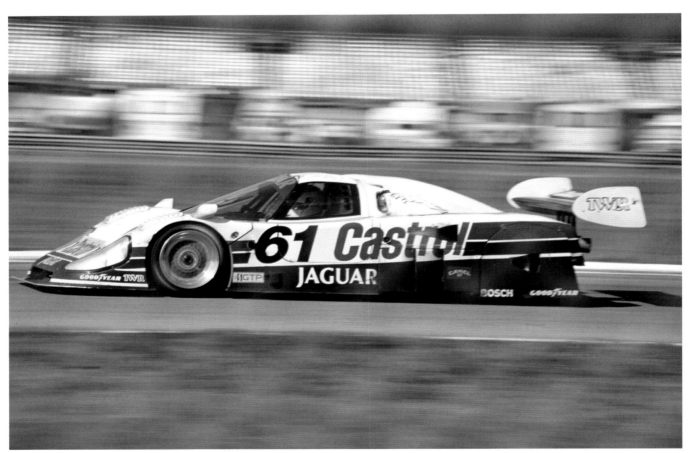

It was smiles all around at Daytona in early February, when the number 61 XJR-12D, chassis 388, of Davy Jones, Jan Lammers and Andy Wallace repeated TWR's victory of 1988. To make things even better, the sister car, 288, of Martin Brundle, Price Cobb and John Nielsen, finished second. (Courtesy Lee Self)

Except for the true long distance races such as the Daytona and Le Mans 24 hours, and the Sebring 12 hours, where reliability was paramount, TWR Jaguar mothballed its V12 engined cars for 1990, now calling them 'XJR-12s,' and concentrated on developing its XJR-10 and -11 cars for the sprint races that comprised the main part of the World Sports Prototype Championship and the IMSA Championship. Ironically, the old V12-engined cars proved to be TWR Jaguar's savior in 1990, where they won at the two 24-hour races, Daytona and Le Mans,

One positive move was the transition from using Dunlop tyres to those made by Goodyear. "Worth at least a second a lap alone," said Tom Walkinshaw, when asked about them.

He also instituted what was called a technical centre, but long time designer Tony Southgate didn't want to be involved in this and left. He was replaced by Ross Brawn, who had previously been with the Arrows F1 team. Brawn concentrated on planning TWR Jaguar's 1991 car, to be powered by a naturally aspirated 3.5-litre Cosworth F1 engine, rather than doing anything more to the XJR-11. Allan Scott, previously in charge of engine design and development, was replaced with an ex-BMW engineer, Gerhard Schumann. He uprated the turbocharged V6 engine to a Bosch 1.7 Motronic ECU, and the cars were now on Goodyear tyres of 17in diameter at the front and 18in at the rear.

Martin Brundle had now returned to TWR after a year of F1, and Jan Lammers and Andy Wallace were sharing one XJR-10, with Alain Ferté to join Martin Brundle in the other.

The season began at Suzuka, Japan on April 8th, and here, Mercedes, now a full factory effort but still with most of the Sauber personnel in the team, rolled out its new, carbon fibre chassis'd (built in England by Dave Price Composites) all-silver C11, another design from Leo Ress: a lower, sleeker version of the previous winning C9. It featured a more powerful engine than the year before, mainly controlled by the new Bosch Motronic 1.8 engine management system. The new Mercedes Group C contender also had a new, stronger gearbox, and the team had switched from Michelin to Goodyear tyres.

The car proved to be quick straight of the box, recording the second quickest time before being crashed on the Saturday afternoon. No problem, Mercedes simply

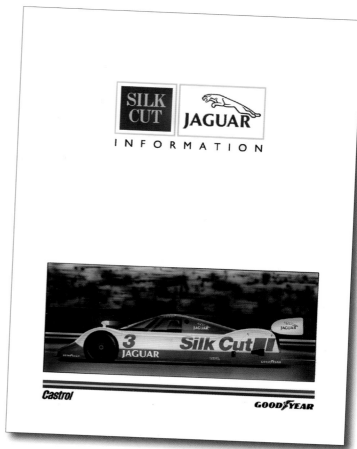

A typical press release cover from TWR. In all things, the team was very professional. (Courtesy John S Allen)

pulled out a spare C9 and occupied the front row of the grid after qualifying was done. TWR Jaguar could do no better than seventh and eighth, as various Japanese and German Turbocharged cars vied for a high place on the grid, whilst TWR concentrated on race setup.

This year, Mercedes had disposed of Kenny Acheson's services, but kept Jean-Louis Schlesser, Mauro Baldi and Jochen Mass. Schlesser and Baldi were teamed together whilst Jochen Mass was to share his car in turn with three young German drivers, Karl Wendlinger, Heinz-Harald Frentzen and a certain Michael Schumacher ...

When the race started, both Mercedes fell back – Mass after a spin on the first lap, and Schlesser started from the pitlane after a last-minute fuel leak was spotted and cured. The TWR Jaguar XJR-11s ran well, Brundle

Race number 3, 490, was the XJR-11 driven by Martin Brundle and Alain Ferté in the Silverstone 1000km. They won, something that TWR made a habit of at its home race. (Courtesy John S Allen)

and Ferté leading at one point but sadly, the oil pumps failed on both cars and they were DNFs at this first race, leaving the Mercedes to cruise home to a one-two victory. A Lola-built Nissan R89C was third, then a works run Toyota 90CV, and a string of Porsche 962s from fourth to tenth.

Monza, with a new-look pits garage and smarter paddock, was next at the end of April, and here the Sauber team fielded two new C11s, which promptly occupied the front row of the grid. The two Jaguars were next and the usual Porsche 962s, the Lola-Nissans and a Spice C1 made up the top ten.

At the lights, it was Jochen Mass again spinning at the entrance to the first corner, at the chicane. He knocked Jan Lammers' XJR-11 off the track, leaving Mauro Baldi with a good lead. When Schlesser took over, Martin Brundle started to catch him, but then brake trouble dropped him back. Karl Wendlinger overtook him to make it another one-two for Mercedes, but at least both Jaguars finished this time, third and fourth.

Things were not looking good for TWR Jaguar, but at Silverstone, Michael Schumacher was disqualified from the race, when, in an unofficial practice session, he stopped at Copse corner, just past the pitlane with a broken gear linkage. The mechanics ran over to help him, in direct opposition to the rule that stated that only a driver could "carry out repairs to the car, using tools or parts carried in the car." So Martin Brundle took second place on the grid and Jan Lammers took third. Mark Blundell's Lola-Nissan was fourth.

In the race itself, the Schlesser/Baldi C11 waltzed off to a 48 second lead but then ... the engine broke. Martin Brundle and Alain Ferté took an emotional win, with Jan Lammers and Andy Wallace second. The Lola-Nissan had challenged for second, but ran out of fuel on the last lap, whilst the C1 Spice took the place. The usual horde of Porsche 962s filled out from fourth place to tenth.

The two Mercedes were truly awesome at Spa-Francorchamps on June 3rd, Mauro Baldi taking pole in 1:59:35, with Jochen Mass second. Behind them, Brundle was third, but he was almost three seconds behind the pole sitter. Jan Lammers was alongside him

The winning Jaguar XJR-11 in its grade at Silverstone in May, just before the race. (Courtesy John S Allen)

to close out the second row. The Lola-Nissan of Mark Blundell was next, after him came Bob Wollek in the Joest-entered Porsche 962, then came the rest ...

On race day, it rained. The kind of misty rain that leaves team managers scratching their heads as to what tyres should be fitted. The Mercedes team opted for intermediates and both cars stayed out to see just what the weather would do. Would the rain return? TWR Jaguar, in the meantime, had gambled that it wouldn't, and Brundle stopped soon after the start to change onto slicks. Jean-Louis Schlesser's Mercedes then had to take

a long pitstop to change an ignition box, but meanwhile Martin Brundle was making hay, shooting off to over a minute's lead by the time the Mercedes pit management had changed the other car, driven by Jochen Mass and Karl Wendlinger, onto slicks as well.

Then Martin Brundle, in the leading XJR-11, smelt burning. The wiring loom had caught fire and he had to stop and retire the leading car. In the other XJR-11, Jan Lammers and Andy Wallace had had to contend with a fuel leak and a seriously oiled-up windscreen. Still, they did manage to finish second to the winning Mercedes,

Number 1 at Le Mans in 1990 was chassis number 990. Driven by Martin Brundle, Alain Ferté and David Leslie, it retired when the water pump on the engine failed. (Courtesy John S Allen)

in which Jochen Mass celebrated his 30th World Championship victory. Julian Bailey and Kenny Acheson finished third in one of the two Lola-Nissans, and the Spice C1 car of Fermín Vélez and Bruno Giacomelli was fourth.

54 cars entered the Le Mans 24 hours, that itself signifying that the ACO wasn't bothered about exclusion from the FISA Championship. Mercedes declined to enter, stating that it hoped its decision might force the ACO and FISA to come to an agreement, but to no avail. Jaguar brought four cars and Lola-Nissan seven.

Julian Bailey used one of them, fitted with a special 'big boost' engine rumoured to develop upwards of 1400 horsepower for one lap only and, considering that the circuit now boasted two chicanes on the Mulsanne straight, posted the incredible time of 3:27:02, fully six seconds faster than anyone had gone before. Martin Brundle, sitting strapped into his TWR Jaguar XJR-12 heard the time and promptly unstrapped himself and climbed out of his car's cockpit. "What's the point?" he asked as the TWR mechanics wheeled his car back to the paddock.

Stand back! One of the XJR-12s seen entering into its pit box during the race. (Courtesy John S Allen)

The crew goes to work. The fuellers are already plugged in and Roger Silman, the team manager with his back to the camera, is directing operations. (Courtesy John S Allen)

The race itself settled down to a TWR Jaguar versus the Lola-Nissans struggle, but all the leading Lola-Nissans fell out with various problems, and the TWR Jaguars had settled into a comfortable one-two when a new challenge arose in the shape of Walter Brun's Porsche 962 in high downforce trim (rather than longtail low downforce trim). The car, driven by Brun himself, Jesus Pareja and Oscar Larrauri, had actually made it to second place with 15 minutes to go when the engine failed, leaving TWR Jaguar first (Martin Brundle, John Nielsen and Price Cobb), and second (Jan Lammers, Andy Wallace and Franz Konrad).

Martin Brundle, when interviewed by *Motorsport* in July, 2019, said: "Tom's plan was for us to drive flat out and draw the Porsches out.

"There were so many, so he was like, 'You go like hell and we'll try and break them.' Then he said, 'and if your car breaks, I'm going to keep your spot in the other car.' Which I think he forgot to mention to poor old Eliseo Salazar.

"I jumped in the other car, run by TWR USA. But that was missing a gear – fourth – and its front brakes had glazed over by that point, so it hadn't got much in the way of retardation, but we got that to the end. I think by the finish I'd done a dozen hours of racing in total.

"The car was overheating. The radiator (in the nose) as you can imagine would get full of debris and rubber. I'll never forget Tom, with a bucket of water, throwing the water through from the other side to try and clear it. So then steam would just envelop you."

At the finish, the track was invaded by some 50,000 British fans, to celebrate the victory. "There was one guy," recalls Martin, laughing, "who was wearing a union flag and apparently, nothing else. Every time we came past, he waved the union flag. I'm pleased to say I didn't see him! They were glorious times, and we had the history of the C Type and the D Type behind us. And in 1988 Jaguar had knocked Porsche from the top spot after six or seven years of dominance."

Continued page 110

As the morning mist is cleared by a rising sun, one of the XJR-12LMs, now sporting a layer of dead insects on its nose, heads towards the afternoon finish. (Courtesy John S Allen)

The winning car at Le Mans in 1990 was race number 3, XJR-12 1090, driven by John Nielsen, Price Cobb, Eliseo Salazar and Martin Brundle. It is seen here being prepared before the race. (Courtesy John S Allen)

... And here it is directly after the finish, with the stewards and pit crew attempting to keep the crowd at bay. (Courtesy John S Allen)

Number 1 at Le Mans in 1990 was chassis number 990. Driven by Martin Brundle, Alain Ferté and David Leslie, it retired when the water pump on the engine failed. (Courtesy John S Allen)

We've won again! Chassis number 1090, driven by Martin Brundle, Price Cobb, John Nielsen and Eliseo Salazar was the winning car at Le Mans in 1990. (Courtesy John S Allen)

Race number 3 at Donington in September was driven by Martin Brundle and Alain Ferté. This was an XJR-11, chassis number 1190, and it was, like the sister car, disqualified for over-fuelling. (Courtesy John S Allen)

The sister car at Donington, XJR-11, chassis number 1290, driven by Jan Lammers and Andy Wallace. (Courtesy John S Allen)

Despite its age and a weight handicap, the Porsche 962 could still put up some good performances, particularly when being run by such a professional team as Joest. (Courtesy John S Allen)

After this, the last four championship races were an anti-climax for the TWR Jaguar team, though they were, usually, the best of the rest behind the all-conquering Mercedes. At the Nürburgring on August 19th, Schlesser and Baldi won outright, with Mass and Schumacher second. Brundle and Ferté were third, but a lap down, and Lammers and Wallace were fourth.

At Donington at the beginning of September, TWR Jaguar suffered a further indignity when both cars were disqualified for taking on too much fuel. It didn't really make much difference to the result, as the two Mercedes had run away with the race anyway, the two silver C11s giving Mercedes the Manufacturers' Championship at this point.

At the next race at Montreal on September 23rd, Jean-Louis Schlesser and Mauro Baldi won outright, giving them the joint Drivers' Championship, despite a manhole cover lifting and part of it going through Jesus Pareja's windscreen on his Porsche 962. The Porsche caught fire and Pareja was lucky to escape with only minor burns, but the 962 was very badly damaged. After this the race was stopped and half points awarded, but it was a moot point for the two TWR Jaguars, who had both retired by this time. The Lola-Nissan R90C of Julian Bailey and Mark Blundell took second place, and its sister car fifth.

Last race of the season was at Mexico City on October 7th, and, as usual, a Mercedes C11 won, but this time, it was the car of Jochen Mass and Michael Schumacher. This was after Schlesser and Baldi had overtaken them for the win, only to be disqualified for taking on too much fuel. Second was the Lola Nissan of Julian Bailey and Mark Blundell again, and Andy Wallace and Davy Jones finished third for TWR Jaguar. The one high spot for them was that Brundle had taken pole position, for once ahead of the Mercedes C11s. Sadly, after a great start into the lead, Martin Brundle was forced to retire with a faulty alternator.

It had been a very mixed year for TWR and Jaguar, but at least they had won two major 24-hour races, Daytona and Le Mans, but neither of these had been against their rival, Mercedes, who had been dominant and won every other race, except for Silverstone.

Roll on 1991, with a free fuel formula.

Over in America, Nissan had started its own company to look after racing, NPTI, which had taken over from Electramotive. The change was mainly in name and premises only, though, as the same drivers, team

manager (Kas Kastner), designer (Trevor Harris), and crew from Electramotive remained.

For 1990, it produced a new car in mid-season called the NPTI-90, to replace the dominant GTP-ZXT, which had won the IMSA Championship for the last two years. In hindsight, most of the people at NPTI believed that if they had stayed with the ZXT car and developed it, it would have been just fast as the NPTI-90 became, but of course, hindsight is always 20/20.

Toyota, in the shape of Dan Gurney's Eagle team also produced a new car for 1990, but simply referred to it as the new 'Eagle.' This design went very much to the lightweight formula that had been introduced by IMSA on a sliding scale of weight to engine capacity. Later on, Nissan tried going down the same path with its NPTI-90/91 but by then, the series itself was winding down.

1990 turned out to be very similar to 1988 for TWR Jaguar in America, the Castrol-sponsored XJR-12s winning the first race, the Daytona 24 hours. Nissan had led until halfway, then retired with engine problems, and Davy Jones, Jan Lammers and Andy Wallace took the win ahead of Martin Brundle, Price Cobb and John Nielsen.

Nissan had its revenge at the Miami street circuit, despite being bested by the new Toyota Eagle to begin with. Sadly for the Eagle, driver Drake Olson then got into a barging match with Bob Wollek, who was driving a Dauer-entered Porsche 962, and the repairs needed to the Toyota allowed Geoff Brabham back into his usual place and to take the win. Davy Jones had been ninth on the grid in his XJR-10, but retired almost straight away when his engine blew.

Derek Daly and Bob Earl drove the winning Nissan at the Sebring 12 hours. The car had placed second the year before. Geoff Brabham and Chip Robinson finished second in a similar car and Davy Jones, Andy Wallace and Jan Lammers were third in an XJR-12. All three finished on the same lap after 12 hours of racing.

Nissan won again at Road Atlanta, but at this race, Price Cobb and John Nielsen gave the team a hard time, taking second place in their XJR-10.

At Palm Beach, both Toyota and TWR Jaguar had faster cars than the Nissan, but the Nissan still won, mainly due to faster pitwork, and the sister car placed second. Price Cobb and John Nielsen took third place, a lap behind.

At last, at Topeka, the Toyota Eagle won, leading from

The winning XJR-12D at Daytona before the start of the 24-hour race. (Courtesy Lee Self)

Chassis number 590 was an XJR-11, usually raced by Andy Wallace and Jan Lammers in 1990. (Courtesy Alan Dike)

By Mid-Ohio in June, the new XJR-10 Turbo cars were doing the IMSA 'Sprint' races. They often proved fragile, as was the case here, with both the number 60 car (589) and the 61 (389) going out with blown engines. (Courtesy Lee Self)

start to finish. The second car entered finished fourth. The XJR-10s were outgunned here, managing to take only fifth and sixth. This race saw the debut of the new Nissan NPTI90, but although qualifying in second place, it could only manage eighth at the finish; its older sister car, a ZXT with Geoff Brabham and Chip Robinson driving, finishing second.

But then came Lime Rock, and at last another Jaguar victory, this time with an XJR-10 driven by Price Cobb and John Nielsen. It beat the next finisher by over a lap. Surprisingly, the Nissans only managed to finish fourth and 14th; the Spices finishing second and third.

In 1989, the XJR-10 had had 6633lb of downforce but, for 1990, the Tony Dowe-led team had raised that to 7181lb, which undoubtedly helped on many of America's short tracks. Also, the often troublesome Zytec engine management system was replaced by Bosch equipment. Just as in Europe, TWR Jaguar changed from

Dunlop as a tyre supplier to Goodyear, another move in the quest for better performance

Mid-Ohio in June was just the reverse: Nissan placing one-two again and both Jaguars retiring before one third distance with blown engines. Geoff Brabham and Derek Daly drove the new NPTI90 to its first victory.

Hurley Haywood and James Weaver drove the Dyson Porsche 962 to second place at Watkins Glen in July, beating out Davy Jones and Alain Ferté in the third-placed XJR-10, which engine had blown on the very last lap. Price Cobb and John Nielsen were fourth. Chip Robinson and Bob Earl in the Nissan won, Geoff Brabham and Derek Daly finishing an uncharacteristic fifth.

At Sears Point two weeks later the Toyota Eagle won, beating the two Nissans into second and third, the XJR-10s finishing in fourth and sixth, all six cars finishing on the same lap. Chevrolet Spices had taken pole and second on the grid, but faded in the race proper.

Need a spare engine sir? The V6 engine of the XJR-10. (Courtesy Lee Self)

On the road or on the track

... the Cats
depend on Castrol
for Maximum Protection.

The Castrol Jaguar race cars are powered by twin turbo V-6 and
V-12 engines and reach speeds in excess of 200 MPH during 3 hour
sprints and grueling 24 hour endurance races. Castrol is the motor
oil that lubricates and protects these high tech machines. And,
Castrol is the only motor oil recommended by Jaguar for their luxury
automobiles worldwide.

Castrol provides maximum protection against viscosity and
thermal breakdown. So, if you demand quality for your automobile,
demand Castrol . . . Jaguar does!

In 1990, Jaguar let Castrol help with its advertising in the IMSA yearbook. (Courtesy IMSA Yearbook)

TWR Jaguar won at a sizzling Portland, Davy Jones withstanding the heat and taking his XJR-10 to a victory over the Toyota Eagle, with a Spice next up. The other XJR-10 was the first retirement, again with a blown engine.

Davy Jones drove another stirring race at Road America three weeks later, but he still could not prevent Geoff Brabham in his Nissan beating him to first place, taking second ahead of Juan Manuel Fangio II in the first Toyota home.

Toyota took another victory at San Antonio in September, Fangio winning again, with the Nissans taking second and third. The Jaguar XJR-10s didn't feature at all, Price Cobb retiring with "mechanical problems," and Davy Jones with accident damage.

Tampa on 30th September saw Porsche's only victory of 1990, James Weaver taking the Dyson 962 to a popular victory over the two Nissans, one a car entered by BF Goodrich and driven by John Paul Jr. John Nielsen was fourth but Davy Jones was out again, this time when the engine blew with just ten laps to run. Pouring rain had turned the result into a toss up of who had the right tyres and could manage the rain the best.

The final race of the IMSA season was on 11th November at Del Mar, and Fangio in the Toyota won again, but this time it was Davy Jones in the XJR-10 in second place, beating John Paul Jr in the first Nissan home. Geoff Brabham was fifth, beating James Weaver in the Dyson 962 and Martin Brundle in the second XJR-10 finished down in 11th after various problems. For the third year in succession, Geoff Brabham and Nissan had taken the Championships.

In Europe, it had been Mercedes that had beaten TWR Jaguar, but in America, it was Nissan and Toyota who were beating them. Something better than the XJR-10 and 11 was needed for 1991.

XJR-9 – 288

1990:
Upgraded to XJR-12D spec
4-6/01: Daytona Tests (as 288)
3-4/02: Daytona 24 hours: P Cobb/J Nielsen/M Brundle, #60; 2nd
17/03: Sebring 12 hours: J Nielsen/P Cobb, #60; DNF (engine)
Renumbered to 1090 (XJR-12LM)
16-17/6: Le Mans 24 hours: J Nielsen/P Cobb/M Brundle/E Salazar, #3; 1st
In TWR collection

2003:
Oct. Sold

XJR-9 388

1990:
3-4/2: Daytona 24 hours: D Jones/J Lammers/A Wallace, #61; 1st
17/3: Sebring 12 hours: D Jones/J Lammers/A Wallace, #61; 3rd
In TWR collection

2003:
October, sold

XJR-9 – 588 (renumbered to 990)

1990:
16-17/6: Le Mans 24 hours: M Brundle/A Ferté/D Leslie, #1; DNF (water pump)

1991:
22-23/6: Le Mans 24 hours: D Jones/R Boesel/M Ferté, #35; 2nd
Sold to Neil Hadfield

XJR-11 – 189

1990:
8/4: Suzuka: M Brundle/M Ferté, #3; DNF (engine)
29/4: Monza: T car
20/5: Silverstone, ~3T; T car
3/6: Spa-Francochamps, T car
22/7: Dijon: T car
Renumbered to 1390, spare car only, not known if attended any race meetings as 1390

1994:
Sold at Coys Historic Festival auction
Sold to Manfred Lipman, USA
In Imperial Palace Collection

XJR-11 – 289

1990:
08/4: Suzuka: J Lammers/A Wallace, #4; DNF (turbo)
29/4: Monza: J Lammers/A Wallace, #4; 4th
Renumbered as 590 for Silverstone race 20/5/90
See details for 590 re: Silverstone, 3/6 Spa and 22/7 Dijon race results

XJR-10 – 389

1990:
25/2: Miami; P Cobb/ J Nielsen, #61; DNR
01/4: Road Atlanta: P Cobb/J Nielsen, #61; 2nd
23/4: W Palm Beach: P Cobb/J Nielsen, #61; 3rd
06/5: Topeka: P Cobb/J Nielsen, #61; 5th
28/5: Lime Rock: P Cobb/ J Nielsen, #61; 1st

3/6: Mid-Ohio: J Nielsen/P Cobb#61; DNF (engine), classified 19th
1/7: Watkins Glen: P Cobb/J Nielsen, #61; 4th
15/7: Sears Point: P Cobb/J Nielsen, #61; 6th
29/7: Portland: J Nielsen/P Cobb, #61; DNF (engine), classified 20th
19/8: Road America: J Nielsen, #61; 6th
02/9: San Antonio: P Cobb, #61; DNF (engine), classified 14th
30/9: Tampa: J Nielsen, #61; 4th
11/11: Del Mar: M Brundle, #61; 11th

XJR-10 – 589

1990:
25/2: Miami GP: D Jones/M Brundle, #60; DNF (engine), classified 26th
01/4: Road Atlanta: D Jones/J Lammers, #60; 7th
22/4: W Palm Beach: D Jones/J Lammers, # 60; DNF (accident), classified 19th
06/5: Topeka: D Jones/M Brundle, # 60; 6th
28/5: Lime Rock: D Jones/J Lammers, #60; DNF (engine/turbo), classified 23rd
3/6: Mid-Ohio: D Jones/P Cobb, #60; DNF (engine) classified 17th
01/7: Watkins Glen: D Jones/A Ferté, #60; 3rd
15/7: Sears Point: D Jones/A Ferté, #60; 4th
29/7: Portland: D Jones, #60; 1st
19/8: Road America: D Jones, #60; 2nd
02/09: San Antonio: D Jones, #60; DNF (accident), classified 20th
30/09: Tampa: D Jones, #60; DNF (driver fatigue), classified 12th
11/11: Del Mar: D Jones, #60; 2nd

XJR-12 – 190

1990:
16-17/6: Le Mans 24 hours: D Jones/M Ferté/E Salazar/ l Perez-Sala, #4; DNF (engine)

XJR-12 – 290

1990:
16-17/6: Le Mans 24 hours: J Lammers/A Wallace/F Konrad, #2; 2nd
7-9/12: Sebring Practice

1991:

3-5/1: Daytona Tests: 1:39:54

2-3/2: Daytona 24 hours: D Jones/S Pruett/R Boesel/D Warwick, #2; DNF (engine), classified 30th

16/3: Sebring 12 hours: D Jones/K Acheson/R Boesel, #2; DNS, crashed in practice by Jones

22-23/6: Le Mans 24 hours: J Krosnoff/D Leslie/M Martini, #36; DNF (gearbox), Suntec XJR-12LM

Car scrapped, chassis damage

390?

Listed as XJR-10 for IMSA

No information available, no race history available

Possible spare chassis intended to replace 489

XJR-11 – 490   3.5-litre twin-turbo   Group C Silk Cut

1990:

29/4: Monza: M Brundle/A Ferté, #3; 3rd

20/5: Silverstone: M Brundle/A Ferté, #3; 1st

03/6: Spa-Francorchamps: M Brundle/A Ferté, #3; DNF (wiring)

22/7: Dijon: M Brundle/A Ferté, #3; 5th

Re-numbered to 1190, for the rest of the 1990 season

19/8: Nürburgring: M Brundle/A Ferté, #3; 3rd

02/9: Donington: M Brundle/A Ferté, #3; DQ (fuel), finished 3rd but disqualified for fuel

23/9: Montreal: M Brundle/J Lammers, #3; 15th DNF (driveshaft)

7/10: Mexico City: M Brundle/J Lammers, #3; DNF (alternator)

XJR-11 – renumbered back to 490 from 1190

1991:

Raced in All Japan Sports Car and Prototype Championship in Suntec livery

Sold to Paul Spires, and won the first ever European historic Group C race

Sold to Don Law, for a client, and raced – with many wins – by Win Percy in Group C – GTP, in Europe

2004:

Sold to Henry Pearman

12/6: Le Mans (Support race): H Pearman, #3; 7th (1st Jaguar)

2005:

STP0

XJR-11 – 590   3.5-litre twin-turbo   Group C Silk Cut (renumbered from 289)

1990:

20/5: Silverstone: J Lammers/A Wallace, #4; 2nd

03/6: Spa-Francorchamps: J Lammers/A Wallace, #4; 2nd

22/7: Dijon: J Lammers/A Wallace, #4; 4th

Re-numbered as 1290 for rest of 1990 season

19/8: Nürburgring: J Lammers/A Wallace, #4; 4th

02/9: Donington: J Lammers/A Wallace, #4; actually finished 8th but disqualified

23/9: Montreal: D Jones/A Wallace, #4; DNF (driveshaft)

7/10: Mexico City: A Wallace/D Jones, #4; 3rd; actually finished 4th but subsequently moved to 3rd

Renumbered back to 590 in 1991 – spare car in AJS&PC sponsored by Suntec

Sold to Derek Hood, JD Classics

2004:

12/6: Le Mans (Support race); G Pearson, #4; Pole, 10th; DNF

Sold to Phil Bennet

XJR-10 – 690

The XJR-16s were converted XJR-10s, updated and modified by Mr Ross Brawn. The 16 with the humped roof was previously XJR10 690 in Castrol colours, sold and used in the interserie by Dieter Bergerman, and entered as XJR16 #690. He later restored the car to XJR10 #690 in Castrol livery and sold it.

8

XJR-10-17 1991-1993

Ross Brawn and his team of 12 designers had done good work on the new 3.5-litre model, with its naturally-aspirated engine. The XJR-14 was a very purposeful, good looking race car, no matter how subjectively one looks at it. In its striking purple Silk Cut livery, it was an immediate race winner. Built around the Cosworth Ford HB 3.5-litre V8, wearing Jaguar badges, and initially rated at some 675 horsepower at 12,800rpm

Above and opposite: The XJR-14, from the team headed by Ross Brawn, was a great car, following in the winning trail of the XJR-6/7/8/9/12. (Courtesy Graham Robson)

(later raised to 735 horsepower at 13,500rpm, with pneumatic valve operation), it still used a chassis made of carbon fibre, but this time it also used aluminium laid underneath. There was no allowance for doors, the drivers being expected to enter and exit the car through the hinged side windows. Even the ducting to the front brake discs was effectively 'cast in' out of carbon fibre

Radiators were mid-mounted, in order to concentrate weight around the centre of the car, with inlets on either side of the cockpit, and there was a roof-mounted air intake supplying air to the engine. The nose was pierced for the brake ducts only, thus allowing for a front wing between the extremities of the front fenders, as the March 82-85gs had featured. This front wing was very much for fine-tuning handling.

At the rear of the body was a huge double tier wing with big endplates. This was a particularly elegant way of using the lower wing to extract air from the underbody ground effect tunnels, whilst the upper tier acted as the actual 'wing' to add/subtract extra downforce as needed.

The front suspension was pushrod operated and acted via torsion bars. A screw jack in the centre of the nose acted on ride height, and springing was altered by changing the diameter of the torsion bars, which were mounted horizontally at the front of the chassis.

Rear suspension was also pushrod operated, but via the more normal springs and damper units. The XJR-14 had very uncluttered venturii. Weight was now below the minimum of 750kg, so that ballast could be added as necessary. The six-speed gearbox's gear cluster itself was in front of the rear axle – another case of weight being kept within the centre of the car – and the starter motor itself operated on the input shaft via a two stage gearbox and clutch. The gear-change was as in a normal streetcar, that is, in the middle of instead of the usual right-hand setup on a race car. This allowed a simpler, more direct linkage, though some of the drivers did not find it easy to adapt to a left-hand change.

The seven-race-only 1991 season suffered from a low entry list even before it had started. The first race was at Suzuka on April 14th, and Derek Warwick blitzed the opposition, posting a fastest lap of over 120mph, going some 2.5 seconds faster than Keke Rosberg could manage in his 'new formula' Peugeot 905 Evo. In the race itself, Warwick led easily until his pitstop, when the starter motor failed, and Martin Brundle's car stopped out on the circuit when water from his drink

bottle found its way onto the XJR-14's electrics. Another new formula Peugeot 905 EVO won, driven by Mauro Baldi and Philippe Alliot. In second place came an 'old formula' ballasted Mercedes C11 of Jean-Louis Schlesser and Jochen Mass, whilst third was taken by a ballasted Porsche 962. Embarrassingly, the new flat 12-engined Mercedes C291 proved to be slower than the old ballasted C11, but both Schlesser and Mass complained of twitchy steering caused by the extra weight.

Once more, at Monza the following month, it was a TWR Jaguar XJR-14 on pole, this time being driven by Teo Fabi. Martin Brundle's XJR-14 had to make an engine change after the morning warm up and start from the pitlane in the race, but he was up to third place by

What a line-up! Looking resplendent in its new purple Silk Cut livery, the TWR team made an impressive showing at Le Mans in 1991. (Courtesy John S Allen)

XJR-12, race number 34, was chassis number 991, and was a freshly built XJR-12 for Le Mans in 1991. These 1991 cars used the 'ultimate' Jaguar V12 engines, now of 7.4-litre capacity. After a shakedown at Silverstone on 24th May, it carried Kenny Acheson, Teo Fabi and Bob Wollek to a fine third place. (Courtesy John S Allen)

the third lap, and took second away from Keke Rosberg in his Peugeot by lap seven. Teo Fabi led easily from the start, but then the pace car was deployed when Max Cohen-Olivar rolled his Porsche 962C, just as Fabi pitted. He needed a new starter motor fitted, which was done but left him in 13th place. The second Jaguar came into the race in second place to Yannick Dalmas in a Peugeot 905 Evo. Dalmas pitted for Rosberg to take over and knocked down a mechanic, thankfully injuring him only slightly, and, in the confusion, so much time was lost that Rosberg exited the pits down in eighth place. At the finish the two TWR Jaguars cruised home in first and second, the C11 of Schlesser and Mass taking third.

So to Silverstone on May 19th, and once again the XJR-14 showed its superiority, the two Jaguars occupying the front row. Even the new Peugeots could not come within four seconds of them. It certainly looked as though, for once, TWR Jaguar had upped its game after being beaten for the last two seasons.

At the start, Teo Fabi drove off into the distance. Martin Brundle missed a gearshift and then had the throttle cable break, putting him well down the order, but setting the scene for a great comeback drive. He charged back to third, demoting the Mercedes C11, and Fabi and Derek Warwick won the race. The Mercedes new formula C291 of Karl Wendlinger and Michael Schumacher finished second.

This year, Le Mans was back as a part of the 'FIA Sports Car Championship of Drivers and Teams,' to give it its full title and the new formula 3.5-litre cars were obliged to run, but neither Jaguar nor Mercedes were serious about using these comparatively fragile cars in the race itself.

Andy Wallace: "The XJR-14 was a great car. In 1991, the first ten slots on the grid were allocated to the 3.5-litre 'Atmo' cars. Of course, it was relatively slow down the straight, making up its lap time in the corners. I remember that we only practised with it at Le Mans as the team reckoned that it had no chance of lasting

Number 4, chassis number 691, at Le Mans in 1991 was the XJR-14, to be driven by Andy Wallace, Teo Fabi and Kenny Acheson. It was withdrawn before the start, and the drivers dispersed to the various XJR-12s that actually took part in the race. (Courtesy John S Allen)

24 hours. We also didn't have a big enough final drive gear ratio for the Mulsanne straight. So here I was, on the rev-limiter on the straight, but when I got to the Porsche curves, I just kept my foot in it and caught up to Jan Lammers in an XJR-12, which slowed me down. When I got back to the pits, the XJR-14s were put away and I was down to drive one of the XJR-12s and finally finished fourth."

Although both the Joest team, with its Porsche 962s, and TWR Jaguar, with its XJR-12s, ran high-downforce bodywork, it was the Mercedes C11s that topped the

times in qualifying, Schlesser piloting his car around in 3:31:27, almost 139mph average.

Four XJR-12s were entered, all running with their engines enlarged to 7.4 litres. A longer stroke of 88.5mm was responsible, together with shorter conrods. Three of the XJR-12s were in purple 'Silk Cut' colors, whilst a fourth was entered by Suntec, a Japanese education and university complex. A dark horse entry was the Mazda team with three four-rotor engine 787s. The team was managed by six-time Le Mans winner, Jackie Ickx. They only had to run at an 830kg weight limit.

Another freshly built car for Le Mans in 1991, XJR-12 891, finished fourth overall, having been driven by John Nielsen, Andy Wallace and Derek Warwick. (Courtesy John S Allen)

The winning car at Le Mans 1991 was this Mazda 787, driven by Johnny Herbert, Johnny Dumfries and Volker Weidler. Driven flat out from the start, it exhibited the highest reliability and speed to head the following three TWR Jaguar XJR-12LMs. (Courtesy John S Allen)

The first ten grid positions were reserved for the new formula 3.5-litre engine cars, even though the pole-sitting Peugeot 905 of Philippe Alliot, Jean-Pierre Jabouille and Mauro Baldi was some three seconds slower than the fastest Mercedes C11 of Schlesser, Jochen Mass and Alain Ferté.

At the 12-hour mark, the C11 driven by Michael Schumacher, Karl Wendlinger and Fritz Kreuzpointer led, ahead of the Schlesser/Mass/Kurt Thiim C11. The third-placed Jaguar was three laps behind, but fourth now was the Johnny Herbert, Volker Weidler and Bertrand Gachot driven Mazda 787, which the trio had been driving flat out from the start of the race.

During the morning, Karl Wendlinger brought in the leading Mercedes with

XJR-14 number 3, chassis number 791 at Le Mans was the spare car of Teo Fabi, which never ran. (Courtesy John S Allen)

gearbox problems, and the mechanics set to. By the time it came out again, it had dropped to ninth place in the running order. Although the leading C11 now had a very long lead, the drivers did not like the message that the temperature gauge was beginning to send.

Not a 'Silk Cut' TWR XJR-12! Suntec from Japan sponsored this XJR-12, chassis number 290. It had finished second in the Daytona 24 hours of 1991. At Le Mans it was driven by Jeff Krosnoff, David Leslie and Mauro Martini, but retired with gearbox problems after 183 laps. (Courtesy John S Allen)

At one o'clock, the leading Mercedes pulled into the pits, its race run. The engine had overheated, due to the bracket supporting the water pump breaking. The Mazda screamed into a lead it would not now lose, with three Jaguar XJR-12s following.

At the finish, Johnny Herbert, the last driver in the Mazda, fainted in his father's arms as he climbed from the winning car, so hard had the trio of young drivers driven to win the race.

Two months later (!) came the next race at the Nürburgring. Martin Brundle had departed TWR for the Brabham F1 team, his place being taken by David Brabham. The Peugeot 905 now appeared with new bodywork strikingly similar to that of the XJR-14, and the improvement was obvious, the new car being only slightly slower than the Jaguar.

Still going strong after all these years. A design originating with the 956 of 1982, the 962, despite being weighted down with extra ballast in 1991, was still the weapon of choice of the wealthy privateer. This one, seen here at Le Mans in 1991, was a joint entry by Joest and Konrad Motorsport. Driven by Louis Krages ('John Winter'), Bernd Schneider and Henri Pescarolo, it failed to finish, covering 197 laps, against the winning Mazda's 362. (Courtesy John S Allen)

The opposition. The Peugeot 905 was the French company's contender in the free fuel, 3.5-litre 'Atmo' year, but it was well outpaced by Ross Brawn's XJR-14. It finally came good in 1992. At Le Mans in 1991, this 905, driven by Keke Rosberg, Yannick Dalmas and Pierre-Henri Raphanel, was out after just 68 laps. (Courtesy John S Allen)

TWR Jaguar were a brilliant team and it was an honor to drive for them. I have great memories of that time. Tom was a hard man, but fair.

ANDY WALLACE

The cover of the programme for the race at Mexico in 1991.
(Courtesy John Gabrial)

The Mercedes C11 and Jaguar XJR14 in the programme for
the race in Mexico. Note how the Jaguar is wrongly identified!
(Courtesy John Gabrial)

Teo Fabi took an immediate lead in the XJR-14, the Peugeots running close behind, but Rosberg was soon out when his Peugeot dropped a valve and he slid off into a gravel trap. David Brabham in the second XJR-14 then inherited the lead when Teo fabi, lapping Jurgen Opperman's 962C, hit him and spun.

Mauro Baldi's Peugeot passed David Brabham, but then Baldi's Mercedes' engine failed, and the race ran out with the XJR-14 of David Brabham and Derek Warwick as the winner, and the sister XJR-14 of Teo Fabi/David Brabham finishing second.

The Peugeot 905 EV14 of Keke Rosberg and Yannick Dalmas won the next two races, at Magny Cours and Mexico City. The best the XJR-14 could do was third, behind another Peugeot at Magny Cours, the Jaguar driven by Teo Fabi and David Brabham. Incidentally, Magny Cours was the circuit where most of the testing of the new Peugeot 905 Evo 1 Bis had been done to make it more competitive. That it had succeeded was beyond doubt!

The final race of 1991 was held at the Autopolis circuit in Japan. Teo Fabi took an XJR-14 and wrung its neck to take pole position, giving him a shot at the Drivers' Championship that Derek Warwick looked like winning at this point. Toyota had brought along its new 3.5-litre contender, the TS010, and this placed fifth on the starting grid.

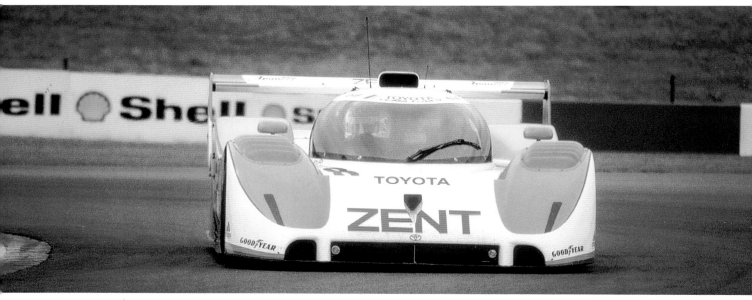

The Toyota TS010 was another stunning design from the pen of Tony Southgate. (Courtesy John S Allen)

Mercedes Group C challenger for 1991, the C291. Using a flat 12 engine of 3.5 litres, it had a troubled start to its career. The engine blocks suffered from being porous. At the race in Mexico, this car, driven by Michael Schumacher, set the fastest lap before oil pump failure forced its retirement. (Courtesy Daimler Chrysler archives)

Yannick Dalmas led at the start, overwhelming Fabi when he missed a gearshift. Schumacher had taken third place in the Mercedes C291, and Warwick was right behind him as these four tore off ahead of the rest of the pack. Schumacher then out-braked Fabi and, as he closed on the leader, Dalmas' engine let go and Michael Schumacher now led the race. Fabi slipped back, concerned with preserving the XJR-14 to the end of the race, whilst staying ahead of Derek Warwick; in the end he had to let him by and settle for third place. Karl Wendlinger took over from Michael Schumacher and Derek Warwick tried hard to overtake the Mercedes, but was continuously held up behind traffic.

So Teo Fabi won the Drivers' Championship with 86 points, Derek Warwick second on 79, and Silk Cut Jaguar won the World Sports Car Championship for the third time on 108 points, with Peugeot second on 79.

Andy Wallace again: "TWR Jaguar were a brilliant team and it was an honour to drive for them. I have great memories of that time. Tom was a hard man, but fair. Mind you, you had to be careful when you negotiated with him for next year's contract. You might leave his office and realise later that you'd settled for less than he'd just paid you!"

Shortly thereafter, Jaguar, whose partnership with TWR had now expired, instructed TWR to send the three XJR-14s to America, where Tony Dowe's team had been fighting for the IMSA Championship with the XJR-16 in 1991 – basically the XJR-10 with a lot of improvements, such as the huge new double tier rear wing, similar to that of the XJR-14 in England. This followed a far more aggressively cut down rear deck on the lengthened-by-4in wheelbase. The rear suspension also was similar to that of the XJR-14, utilising pushrods for actuation of the conventional spring/damper units.

Although the concept for the XJR-16 had been started in England by TWR, the work was then transferred to Valparaiso in America, the TWR team's home base there, where the engineers could concentrate on things like ensuring the turbocharged engine received enough cooling, as racing in America involves much higher temperatures than in Europe.

The two long-distance races in America, the Daytona 24 hours and the Sebring 12 hours, were won by,

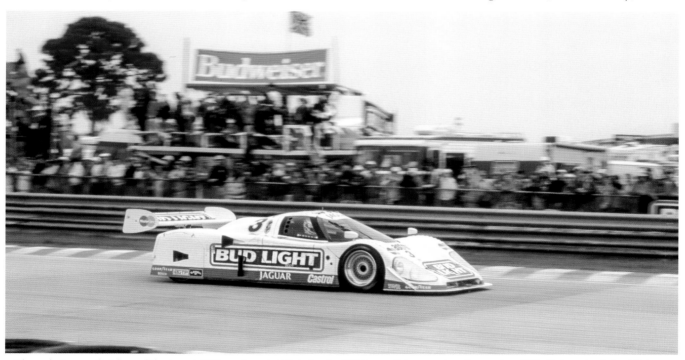

The sole Jaguar finisher of the two J-12Ds entered at Sebring in 1991 was this car, chassis number 190. Driven by John Nielsen, Davy Jones and Raul Boesel, it finished fifth. The sister car was crashed in practice, and the entry withdrawn. (Courtesy Lee Self)

Road Atlanta, April 1991: The parade lap was headed by Raul Boesel in Jaguar XJR-10, race number 3, 589, whilst the car to his right, driven by Davy Jones was a new XJR-16, which won the race outright. (Courtesy Lee Self)

respectively, a Joest-entered Porsche 962 and a Nissan NPTI90. The best that an XJR-12 could do, in either race, was fifth place at Sebring.

The first sprint race for an XJR-10 in 1991 was at West Palm Beach on the 3rd March. Davy Jones led from start to finish, leading all but one lap. Seven different chassis/engine combinations finished in the top seven there, showing how diverse the entry had become.

At the Miami Grand Prix in April, an XJR-10 won again, this time driven by Raoul Boesel. It seemed as if Nissan had some real opposition this year, as a Chevrolet Intrepid had placed second, ahead of Geoff Brabham's Nissan.

Road Atlanta saw the introduction of the XJR-16 and Davy Jones won at an average speed of nearly 121mph.

Chip Robinson finished second in his Nissan NPTI90,

on the same lap as the XJR-16, and Raul Boesel was third, in an XJR-10.

Davy Jones: "The turbocharged V6 engined XJR-10 was heavy and the Intrepid was lighter, they were tough competition. With the XJR-16, that was an improvement (over the XJR-10-Author), and the races had become mainly one driver sprint races, which helped."

There was excitement aplenty at Topeka's Heartland Park, where Davy Jones in his XJR-16 and Wayne Taylor in his Intrepid ran nose to tail for 40 laps. Towards the finish, Chip Robinson got past the Intrepid and then Jones spun on the penultimate lap, leaving the Nissan to win.

Chip Robinson won again for Nissan in his NPTI90 at the next race at Lime Rock, in Connecticut. The Intrepids of Wayne Taylor and Tommy Kendall, plus the XJR-16

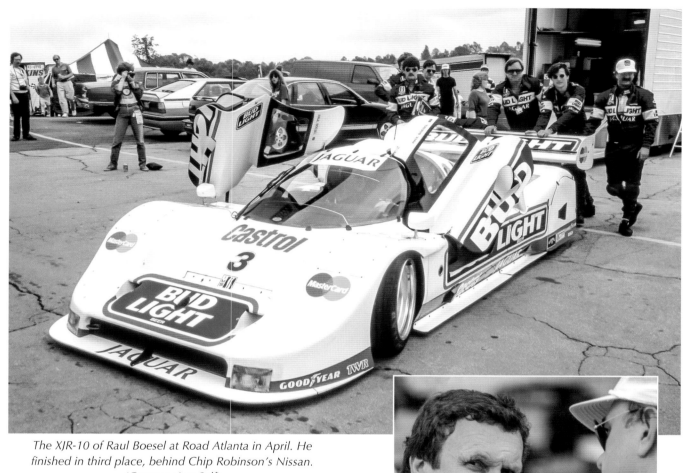

The XJR-10 of Raul Boesel at Road Atlanta in April. He finished in third place, behind Chip Robinson's Nissan. (Courtesy Lee Self)

Tom Walkinshaw in conversation with American TWR Team Manager, Tony Dowe, at Road Atlanta, April 1991.

of Davy Jones, all led in the early running, but all had accidents. The Toyota Eagle of Juan Manuel Fangio II was second, and Geoff Brabham was third, with the two Jaguar XJR-16s of Jones and Boesel finishing sixth and seventh.

Davy Jones posted another victory at Mid-Ohio in June, but those Chevrolet Intrepids of Taylor and Kendall finished on the same lap; Boesel in the second XJR-16 taking fourth.

At last, Intrepids took victory in a rain-shortened race, on the street circuit of New Orleans, Wayne Taylor driving. Geoff Brabham was second and Geoff Purner's

At Jaguar, We Do Some Of Our Best Thinking At Over 200mph.

Innovative thinking. It's the essential ingredient in developing the optimum balance of engine performance, suspension technology, braking ability and chassis design that characterizes Jaguar race cars.

It is the kind of thinking that enabled us to win the 1991 World Sportscar Championship and take more victories in America's prestigious IMSA Camel GTP series than any other marque.

Through the years, technology developed for the track, tested and proven on the great race courses of the world, has benefitted all of our road cars. Today, every Jaguar features four-wheel, anti-lock disc brakes and a fully-independent suspension system employing anti-dive and anti-squat geometry.

You'll find Jaguar's racing spirit embodied in our powerplants as well. From the 223-horsepower,

six-cylinder, 24-valve engine in our Jaguar XJ6, Sovereign, Vanden Plas and Majestic sedans, to the overhead cam, V-12 powerplant in our XJS coupe and convertible, Jaguar engines are truly legendary.

Test drive a Jaguar and discover a car that employs some of our best thinking. For your nearest dealer call 1-800-4-JAGUAR.

J A G U A R

A   B L E N D I N G   O F   A R T   A N D   M A C H I N E

Once again, Jaguar missed no opportunity to advertise the TWR Jaguars' success in IMSA racing in America.
(Courtesy IMSA Yearbook)

The XJR-16 of Davy Jones at Road America in August 1991. Davy headed every practice session, qualified on pole, and led from start to finish. (Courtesy Lee Self)

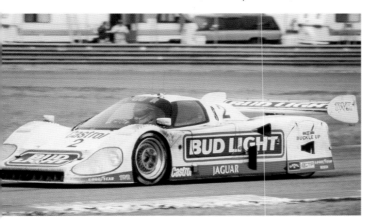

Winners again ... At Daytona for the 24-hour race there in February, 1992, chasing number 891, driven by Davy Jones, David Brabham, Scott Pruett and Scott Goodyear finished in second place, winning the GTP class. (Courtesy Lee Self)

Chevrolet-engined Spice was third. Both XJR-16s retired with suspension damage.

Toyota took a turn on the winner's rostrum of Watkins Glen at the end of June, Fangio taking the victory, with Geoff Brabham second, Chip Robinson third. Boesel was out early on after an accident and Davy Jones only managed 13th. Sadly, Tommy Kendall had a big accident in his Intrepid, and spent the rest of the season recovering from his injuries.

Davy Jones bounced back at Laguna Seca, California on 21st July. Geoff Brabham was second and Englishman Perry McCarthy was third, in a Chevrolet engined Spice. The new Toyota Eagle Mark III debuted here and led, but a penalty for leaving the pits against a red light gave Jones the lead. This really was a season of changes in the order ...

Toyota Eagles were first and third at Portland, the drivers being Fangio and Rocky Moran, respectively. Geoff Brabham came second. The XJR-16 of Davy Jones finished 16th.

Davy Jones won again at the very fast road circuit of Road America, which was the next race. Raul Boesel was fourth in the second team car. Chip Robinson was second, Wayne Taylor third. Geoff Brabham crashed his Nissan in testing and his injuries kept him out of the race and away from the track until the last race at Del Mar.

Suddenly, it seemed, it was last race time at Del Mar in California, nearly two months after Road America, in October; Fangio in the Toyota Eagle won here, with John Paul Jr in a Pontiac engined Spice second and a recovering Geoff Brabham third; The best XJR-16 result was Martin Brundle in fourth, Davy Jones being well down in 13th place with mechanical problems.

Despite having only won one race, Geoff Brabham was Champion yet again, owing to the points gained by his consistent top five finishes. Chip Robinson finished second in the Championship, just five points behind Brabham's haul of 175 and Davy Jones was third with 158.

1992: IMSA Races

Now that there was no longer any Group C racing in Europe, the XJR-14s were sent over to TWR's base at Valparaiso, near to Indianapolis, to be repainted in Castrol colours. They needed a new exhaust system to drop the car's 130-decibel scream down to the IMSA mandated 108 decibels, but, strangely, this actually helped performance, improving mid-range torque. The roof-mounted air intake was also a no-no where IMSA was concerned, so it went, with two periscopes on the rear deck taking its place, à la XJR-16. Of course, the XJR-14s were to be used in the sprint races only, the dear old XJR-12s being dusted off and prepared for yet another Daytona 24 hours and Sebring 12 hours.

Having failed to place at the Daytona 24 hours in 1991, the XJR-12s, basically a seven year old design now, repaid the faith of their pit and driving crew and finished second overall and took victory in the Camel GT class. Drivers were Davy Jones, David Brabham, Scott Pruett, and Scott Goodyear. Only the one TWR XJR-12D was entered.

A Group C specification Lola-Nissan R91CP took overall victory at Daytona with Masahiro Hasemi, Kazayoshi Hoshino and Toshio Suzuka behind the wheel.

The 23rd February saw the XJR-14 have its first race in America and it created a sensation, screaming around the street circuit of Miami in the lead for many laps with Davy Jones driving, until mechanical problems sidelined it just eight laps from the finish. It was still classified sixth in the results, though. Geoff Brabham gained his first victory in over a year, Wayne Taylor was next, and Chip Robinson was third.

Davy Jones again: "My favourite TWR Jaguar? That had to be the XJR-14. What a car. So much downforce; and light, 16,750 pounds. Although it was 10-15mph slower at the end of any straight, you could make that up in the corners. It was a car that you had to keep your foot down in to get the best out of it; if you backed off, the nose would start to rise… But it was great to know that you were driving a car that had an engine that the boys at Benetton had built up and that it was exactly the same as the engine that had been in Michael Schumacher's F1 car the weekend before.

"My overriding memory of racing with TWR? The fact that the team always had the best people and technology that money could buy and that Tom Walkinshaw always

TWR in England sent its Ross Brawn designed 3.5-litre 'Atmo' XJR-14 to America, and at Road Atlanta it pulverised the opposition, Davy Jones leading from start to finish and setting a new lap record of 134.563mph. (Courtesy Lee Self)

had the best drivers, people like Martin Brundle and Derek Warwick. When you climbed into that cockpit, you knew that everyone else had done their best and now it was up to you ..."

TWR wheeled out its sole TWR Jaguar XJR-12D available for the Sebring 12 hours, and, with Davy Jones and David Brabham driving, finished fourth, 22 laps behind the winning Toyota Eagle of Juan Fangio II and Andy Wallace. Geoff Brabham, Derek Daly and Arie Luyendyk were second in an NPTI90 and Gianpiero Moretti, Massimo Sigala, Oscar Sigala and Bernd Schneider guided a MOMO Porsche 962C to third place.

At Road Atlanta, long a 'Jaguar' track, Davy Jones did it again, taking the XJR-14 to victory ahead of Tommy Kendall in the Intrepid. They were the only two finishers on the lead lap. Francois Migault, from Le Mans in France, together with Hugh Fuller, brought the Applebee's-sponsored Chevrolet Spice into third place. Both Chip Robinson's and Geoff Brabham's Nissans were very badly damaged in separate high speed accidents after tyres failed on each car. Luckily, neither driver was seriously injured, but it left the team with only one car for the next few races, and put the previously dominant team on the back foot.

It was positions reversed at Lime Rock in May, Davy Jones having an accident after just 14 laps that put him out of contention and the car needing a new chassis. Fangio won, Geoff Brabham and Chip Robinson second, Pete Halsmer in a Mazda RX-792P third.

Mid-Ohio and Jones did it again in the rain, winning comfortably in another XJR-14 that had been shipped out of England the Monday before, prepared and sent to the circuit ready to race. Only the Toyota Eagle of Fangio finished on the same lap, but Geoff Brabham still took third place.

On the street circuit of New Orleans, Fangio drove his Toyota Eagle to victory at the next race, just ahead of Geoff Brabham in the sole NPTI90, with the second Toyota of PJ Jones third. Davy Jones was fourth. This was hardly a surprising result, as TWR Jaguars competitors had lobbied the IMSA organisers hard that the car was too light and so, starting at New Orleans, 50lb of extra weight was added to the car. It did not help the handling and probably cost TWR Jaguar the championship.

Now the Toyotas were really in a winning groove, doing it again at Watkins Glen, by no less than five laps but another Japanese manufacturer came second, Price Cobb driving the Mazda RX-792P there, with Davy Jones in third place.

It was another victory for Davy Jones at Mid-Ohio in May, despite the wet conditions. (Courtesy Lee Self)

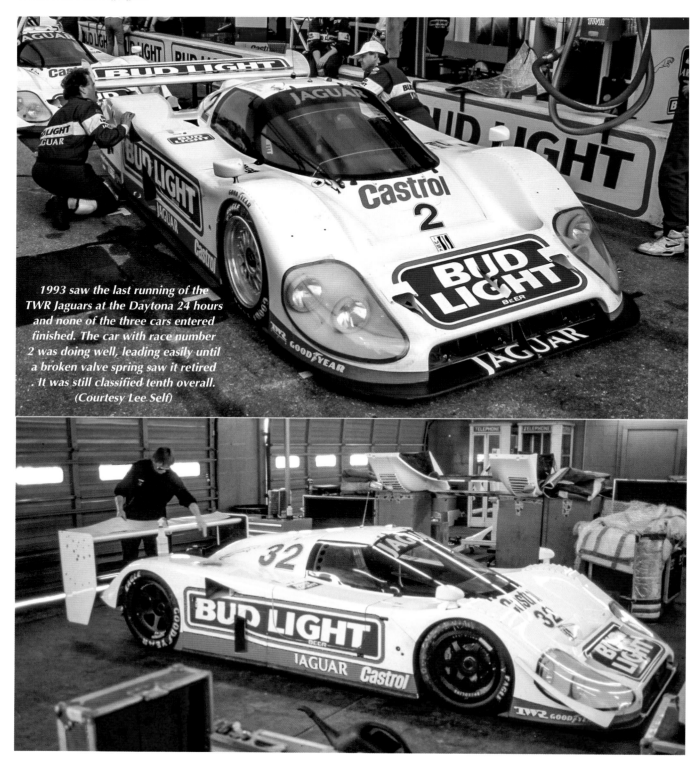

1993 saw the last running of the TWR Jaguars at the Daytona 24 hours and none of the three cars entered finished. The car with race number 2 was doing well, leading easily until a broken valve spring saw it retired. It was still classified tenth overall. (Courtesy Lee Self)

At Laguna Seca, Fangio won again in the Toyota, PJ Jones in the sister car took second, and Davy Jones was third.

Portland, Road America, Phoenix and Del Mar were the final four races. At each one the Toyota Eagles won, coming one-two at the first two races. Davy Jones did his best, but he crashed in the morning warm up at Road America and the team were non-starters. However, Davy took third at Del Mar but the team had been hobbled by the extra weight added to the car. In the end, TWR finished in third place in the IMSA Championship in 1992, a huge disappointment for Jaguar.

Eddie Cheever: "Tom was the outstanding memory of our Jaguar years. Might be the best owner I have ever driven for. He always delivered the best equipment and the team had his full attention. Always."

That was the end for the GTP era for IMSA. A new series called World Sports Cars was introduced in 1993. Gone were pure racing engines and turbochargers, with stock blocks mandated instead. Ground effects were all but eliminated, and the minimum weight ran from 1650 to 2050lb, depending on which engine type/displacement was used. Those were the main points of a 'dumbed down for cheapness' era.

John Fitzpatrick: "You have to admire what Tom Walkinshaw did. He put together a big, and very successful organisation, and to go and win twice at Le Mans and the Daytona 24 hours, as well as the World Champions he gained for Jaguar, was something very special."

After their TWR Jaguar life, two XJR-14s were sold to Mazda and, with Mazda-badged Judd 3.5-litre MV10 engines substituted, became the Mazda MXR-01.

Probably the most amazing result of the XJR-14's design was that Reinhold Joest bought one from TWR America, cut off the roof as per the revised regulations, slotted in a Porsche 962 water/water 3.0 twin turbo engine, called it the WSC-95, and won Le Mans 24 hours outright in 1996 and 1997. That car went into Joest's private collection

There was one more TWR Jaguar race car: the XJR-17. The 17 was a race car first of all, intended for the Camel Lights series for Andy Evans, and made by taking an XJR-16 and removing the turbochargers, thus making the V6 engine naturally aspirated, and also adopting other modifications, such as the rear wing from an XJR-12, the front wing from the XJR-14 design, and tunnels from the

XJR-11 design. The radiators were side mounted, fed by NACA ducts.

Andy Evans, later to buy IMSA, dropped out of the deal before the car was finished. Hugh Chamberlain later wanted it for Le Mans, but could not raise the necessary money.

389

1991:
3/3: West Palm Beach: R Boesel, #3; DNF (transmission) classified 19th
7/4: Miami: R Boesel, #3; 1st

1997:
October: At Valparaiso.
Sold to Don Law, and on to client
Races in Group C – GTP in Europe

589

1991:
03/3: W. Palm Beach: D Jones, #2; 1st
07/4: Miami GP: D Jones, #2; DNF. (engine) Classified 22nd
28/4: Road Atlanta: R Boesel, #3; 3rd
05/5: Heartland Park, Topeka: R Boesel, #3; DNF (mechanical) classified 13th
27/5: Lime Rock: T-Car. Damaged in practice, did not race
Sold to Derek Hood, JD Classics, UK

XJR-12 – 190

1991:
2-3/2: Daytona 24 hours: J Nielsen/K Acheson/E Cheever, #3; DNS (acc)
Nielsen crashed in practice, raced as Bud Light XJR-12D
16/3: Sebring 12 hours: D Jones/R Boesel/J Nielsen, #3; 5th

1993

30-31/1: Daytona 24hrs: S Goodyear/D Jones/S Pruett, #2; DNF classified 10th, raced as Bud Light XJR-12D
In TWR Collection
Sold

2004:

12/6: Le Mans (support race) : J Law; 11th

2014:
With David Clark. £1.8m

XJR-12 – 290

1991:
3-5/1: Daytona Tests: 1:39.54
2-3/2: Daytona 24 hours: D Jones/S Pruett/R Boesel/D Warwick, #2; DNF (engine), classified 30th
16/3: Sebring 12 hours: D Jones/K Acheson/R Boesel, #2; DNS, crashed in practice by Jones
22-23/6: Le Mans 24hrs: J Krosnoff/D Leslie/M Martini, #36; DNF (gearbox) Suntec XJR-12LM
Car scrapped – chassis damage

XJR-11 – renumbered back to 490 from 1190

1991:
Raced in All Japan Sports Car and Prototype Championship in Suntec livery
Sold to Paul Spires, and won the first ever European historic Group C race
Sold to Don Law, for a client, and raced – with many wins – by Win Percy in Group C – GTP, in Europe

2004:
Sold to Henry Pearman
12/6: Le Mans (Support race): H. Pearman, #3; 7th (1st Jaguar)

2005:
STP0

XJR-10 – 690

The XJR-16s were converted XJR-10s updated and modified by the Ross Brawn design team and the Tony Dowe-led TWR team at Valparaiso, USA. The 16 that had the humped roof was previously XJR-10 690 in Castrol colour. This was sold and used in the interserie by Dieter Bergerman, entered as XJR16 #690. He later restored the car back to XJR10 #690 in Castrol livery.

XJR-16 –191 3-litre Twin turbo   IMSA   BUD LIGHT

1991:
28/04: Road Atlanta: D Jones, #2; 1st
05/05: Topeka: D Jones, #2; 2nd
27/05: Lime Rock: D Jones, #2; 7th

02/06: Mid-Ohio: D Jones, #2; 1st
16/06: New Orleans: D Jones, #2; DNF (susp)
30/06: Watkins Glen: D Jones, #2; 13th
21/07: Laguna Seca: D Jones, #2; 1st
28/07: Portland: D Jones, #2; 5th.
25/08: Road America: D Jones, #2; 1st
13/10: Del Mar: D Jones, #2; 13th

1992:
1-2/02: Daytona 24 hours: D Jones/S Goodyear, #3; withdrawn

1997: At Valparaiso
In UK Don Law, raced by Win Percy

2004:
12/06: Le Mans (Support Race): #2; DNF
Sold, raced in Group C – GTP, in Europe

XJR-16 – 291   3-litre Twin turbo   IMSA   BUD LIGHT

1991:
27/05: Lime Rock: R Boesel, #3; 6th.
02/06: Mid-Ohio: R Boesel, #3; 4th.
16/06: New Orleans: R Boesel;#3; DNF (susp)
30/06: Watkins Glen: R Boesel. #3; DNF (acc)
25/08: Road America: R Boesel, #3; 4th
13/10: Del mar: M Brundle, #3; 4th
Converted to naturally aspirated engine, XJR 17 with no known chassis number
Sold on

391

No known car

491

No known car officially
A Mr Chatfield bought this car and it was completed by David Appleby. Don Law has had a chassis plate made for the car, which reads XJR16 #491. This car was created from a brand new turbo chassis, and has a humped roof.

XJR-14 – 591   Delivered 20 Feb 1991
3.5-litre HB Formula 1 engine   Group C

1991:
14/04: Suzuka: D Warwick/M Brundle, #3; 10th. DNF (starter)
05/05: Monza: M Brundle/D Warwick/ T Fabi, #3; 1st.
19/05: Silverstone: M Brundle/D Warwick, #3; 3rd.
22-23/06: Le Mans 24 hours: #3; DNP; Withdrawn
18/08: Nürburgring: T car only
15/09: Magny Cours: T car only
27/10: Autopolis: D Warwick, #3; 2nd; taken as T car but used in race when tank failed on 791
03/11: Sugo, AJS-PC race; taken as T car but had some running by David Brabham

1992:
IMSA
19/07: Laguna Seca: Luyendyk,#3; 4th.
09/08: Road America: D Jones, #2; acc (crashed in race warm-up) Repaired by Astec

2003:
Sold to Phil Bennet, USA

2006:
Sold to Aaron Hsu

2010:
Sold to Gareth Evans

XJR-14 – 691   Delivered 12th March 1991
3.5-litre HB Formula 1 engine   Group C

1991:
14/04: Suzuka: M Brundle/T Fabi, #4; DNF (electrical)
05/05: Monza: T Fabi/M Brundle, #4; 2nd
19/05: Silverstone: T Fabi/D Warwick, #4; 1st
22-23/06: Le Mans 24 hours: A Wallace, #4; DNS.(withdrawn)
18/08: Nürburgring: T Fabi/D Brabham, #4; 2nd
15/09: Magny-Cours: T Fabi/D Brabham, #4; 3rd
06/10: Mexico City: T Fabi/D Brabham, #4; DNS (engine)
27/10: Autopolis, Japan: T Fabi/D Brabham, #34 #4; 3rd
03/11: Sugo, Japan, AJS-PC: D Brabham, #17; 1st
Renumbered as #192

1992:
IMSA
31/05: Mid-Ohio: D Jones, #2; 1st
14/06: New Orleans: D Jones, #2; 4th
28/06: Watkins Glen: D Jones, #2; 3rd

19/07: Laguna Seca: D Jones, #2; 3rd
26/07: Portland: D Jones, #2; DNF (mech)
04/10: Phoenix: D Jones, #2; 2nd
11/11: Del Mar: D Jones, #2; 3rd DNF (mech); not running at finish
Renumbered back to #691
Became Joest-Porsche. WSC95 001 10 1994, raced at Le Mans in 1996 and 1997 by the Joest Porsche team, winning the race on both occasions. Now in Reinhold Joest's private museum

XJR-14 – 791   Delivered 10th May 1991

1991:
18/08: Nürburgring: D Brabham/D Warwick, #3; 1st
15/09: Magny Cours. David Brabham /D Warwick, #3; 5th
06/10: Mexico City: D Brabham/D Warwick, #3; 6th
27/10: Autopolis, Japan: D Brabham/D Warwick, #3; not raced, tank failed, 591 used instead
03/11: Sugo, Japan (AJC-PC): J Krosnoff/M Martini, #18; 9th

1992
#2 IMSA-Jones
23/02: Miami: D Jones, #2; DNF
26/04: Rd Atlanta: D Jones, #2; 1st
26/05: Lime Rock: D Jones, #2; DNF (acc)

1994:
Back to TWR for new tub
In TWR collection

2003:
STP0

XJR-12
Group C & IMSA GTP 1990-91. Special endurance version of the XJR-6/8/9 V12 built for the Daytona and Le Mans 24-hour races. IMSA version ran with 6.0-litre engine and the Group C with 7.0-litre. First race and win at Daytona, February 3rd/4th 1990 where the cars finished 1-2 and Jones/Lammers/Wallace were the victors. 1-2 win repeated at Le Mans June 16th/17th 1990 (Nielsen/Cobb/Brundle).

The cars returned to Daytona in 1991 with 6.5-litre engines allowed by IMSA rule changes. One was written-off in practice and the other retired after repeated water pump replacements. (Note: All TWR V12 XJRs were raced at Le Mans between 1986-88 in some form of 'low-drag' endurance trim). Sponsors: Castrol.

XJR-12– 891

1991:
22-23/06: Le Mans 24 hours; D Warwick/J Nielsen/A Wallace, #33; 4th

1992:
1-2/02: Daytona 24 hours: D Jones/S Pruett/D Brabham/ S Goodyear, #2; 2nd & 1st in GTP class
21/03: Sebring 12 hours: D Jones/D Brabham, #2; 4th
In TWR Collection

2003:
Sold to Derek Hood, JD Classics

2004
12/6: Le Mans (Support race) #333; DNF
Sold to Peter Garrod, 1.7m Purple

XJR-12 – 991   See renumbered from 188

XJR-12D 193   LWT special

1993:
Silverstone tests
31/1-01/02: Daytona 24 hours: D Jones/J Andretti/D Brabham/J Nielsen, #32; DNF (handling problems)
Sold to Don Law UK
Sold to Nick Lynney

2004:
Le Mans (Support race): #32; DNF

2005:
Continued to race in Group C – GTP racing in Europe

Jaguar data courtesy of Henry Pearman

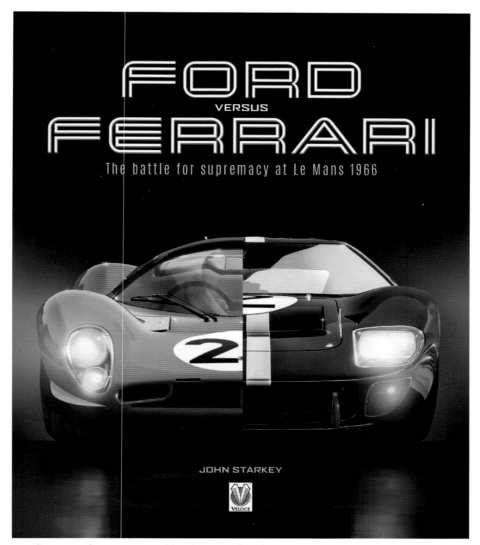

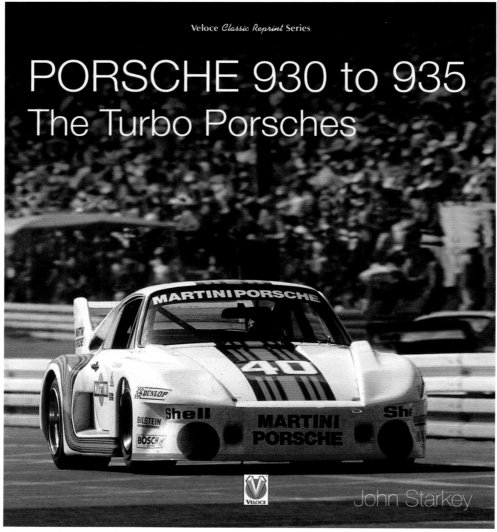

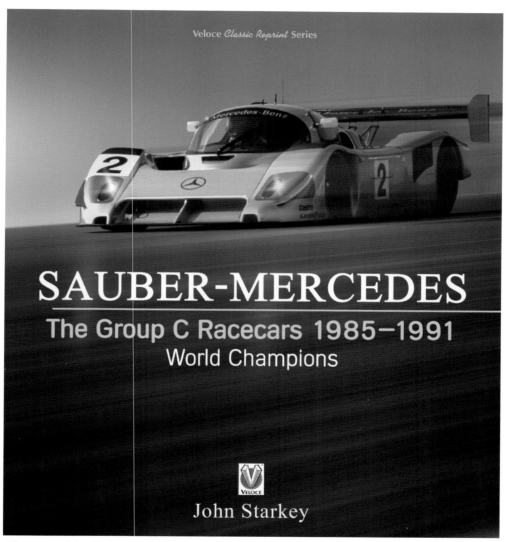

Veloce *Classic Reprint* Series

SAUBER-MERCEDES
The Group C Racecars 1985–1991
World Champions

John Starkey

The story of the Sauber-Mercedes racecars that dominated the Group C racing scene during the late 1980s and early 1990s, covering their design and development. This book features some great colour photos, interviews with many of the best known personalities of the era, and a chassis-by-chassis history of each car.

ISBN: 978-1-787114-93-7
Paperback • 22.8x20.8cm • 128 pages

Email: info@veloce.co.uk • Tel: +44(0)1305 260068

Also from Veloce Publishing –

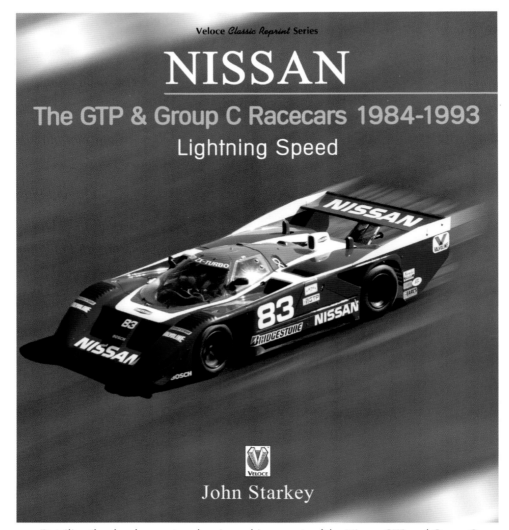

Detailing the development and racing achievements of the Nissan GTP and Group C
racecars. The book features revealing interviews with some of the notable drivers and
designers involved, and, to complete the story, a detailed appendix covering the history of
each car.

ISBN: 978-1-787114-94-4
Paperback • 22.8x20.8cm • 160 pages

For more information and price details, visit our website at www.veloce.co.uk
• email: info@veloce.co.uk • Tel: +44(0)1305 260068

INDEX